CRE⌂TIVE
HOMEOWNER®

landscaping with
stone

PAT SAGUI

TECHNICAL EDITOR FOR
UPDATED EDITION: MARK WOLFE

CREATIVE HOMEOWNER®

Landscaping with Stone, Third Edition (2025) is a revised edition of *Landscaping with Stone, 2nd Edition (2009)*, published by Creative Homeowner, an imprint of Fox Chapel Publishing Company, Inc.

Lanscaping with Stone, Third Edition
Managing Editor: Gretchen Bacon
Editor: Christa Oestreich
Technical Editor: Mark Wolfe
Designer: Chris Morrison, Mike Deppen
Additional Photography: Debbie Wolfe

ISBN 978-1-58011-872-9

Library of Congress Control Number: 2022945995

We are always looking for talented authors. To submit an idea, please send a brief inquiry to acquisitions@foxchapelpublishing.com.

Printed in China
First Printing

Creative Homeowner®, *www.creativehomeowner.com*, is an imprint of New Design Originals Corporation and distributed in North America by Fox Chapel Publishing Company, Inc., 800-457-9112, 903 Square Street, Mount Joy, PA 17552.

ACKNOWLEDGMENTS

Masons, landscape architects, designers, sculptors, and homeowners graciously contributed projects and their hard-earned experience to this book. I am deeply indebted and grateful to them. I am also indebted to the landscape architects and educators whose books inspired and helped me distill a vast body of know-how into a "how-to" primer. To Managing Editor Fran Donegan, who came on the scene after the manuscript was complete, my sincere appreciation for his patience with a first-time author. Special thanks to Charlie Proutt and Danny Young for reading the manuscript and making suggestions to improve it; to Miranda Smith for her tutelage; and to Brian and Will for their good humor and understanding, without which I could not take on projects that add unimagined wanderings to our life.

SAFETY FIRST

All projects and procedures in this book have been reviewed for safety; still it is not possible to overstate the importance of working carefully. What follows are reminders for plant care and project safety. Always use common sense.

- *Always* use caution, care, and good judgment when following the procedures in this book.

- *Always* determine locations of underground utility lines before you dig, and then avoid them by a safe distance. Buried lines may be for gas, electricity, communications, or water. Contact local utility companies who will help you map their lines.

- *Always* read and heed tool manufacturer instructions.

- Always ensure that the electrical setup is safe; be sure that no circuit is overloaded and that all power tools and electrical outlets are properly grounded and protected by a ground-fault circuit interrupter (GFCI). Do not use power tools in wet locations.

- *Always* wear eye protection when using chemicals, sawing wood, pruning trees and shrubs, using power tools, and striking metal onto metal or concrete.

- *Always* consider nontoxic and least toxic methods of addressing unwanted plants, plant pests, and plant diseases before resorting to toxic methods. Follow package application and safety instructions carefully.

- *Always* read labels on chemicals, solvents, and other products; provide ventilation; heed warnings.

- *Always* wear a hard hat when working in situations with potential for injury from falling tree limbs.

- *Always* wear appropriate gloves in situations in which your hands could be injured by rough surfaces, sharp edges, thorns, or poisonous plants.

- *Always* protect yourself against ticks, which can carry Lyme disease. Wear light-colored, long-sleeved shirts and pants. Inspect yourself for ticks after every session in the garden.

- *Always* wear a disposable face mask or a special filtering respirator when creating sawdust or working with toxic gardening substances.

- *Always* keep your hands and other body parts away from the business end of blades, cutters, and bits.

- *Always* obtain approval from local building officials before undertaking construction of permanent structures.

- *Never* employ herbicides, pesticides, or toxic chemicals unless you have determined with certainty that they were developed for the specific problem you hope to remedy.

- *Never* allow bystanders to approach work areas where they might by injured by workers or work site hazards.

- *Never* work with power tools when you are tired, or under the influence of alcohol or drugs.

- *Never* carry sharp or pointed tools, such as knives or saws, in your pocket.

CONTENTS

INTRODUCTION

THIS BOOK IS FOR THE HOMEOWNER who wants to include natural stone in his or her landscape design. More than ever before, the availability of different types of stone and the ease of renting stone-moving equipment make ambitious projects possible—even for homeowners who have no experience working with stone as a landscaping material.

Stone can be used to great effect in all landscapes. For thousands of years, it has served our needs and our fancy. Craftsmen have quarried, hauled, stacked, shaped, laid, mortared, set, shimmed, and carved stone with a breadth of craft and ingenuity that is both awe inspiring and humbling. Those projects are an inspiration to all homeowners who want to include stonework in their designs.

It only makes sense that stone projects should include steps to protect property. In an era of increasing climate uncertainty, intense storms and severe droughts have become more common. These weather and climate events directly impact homes and landscapes by elevating the risk of floods and wildfires. Just as these projects appeal to the senses of beauty and order, well-planned stonework can also improve rainwater infiltration, reduce storm runoff volume and velocity, and act as a firebreak.

► **Mortared flagstone steps** lead up to rustic wood doors at this California home's entryway.

▼ **Stone pavers** set in a star pattern surround a tree on this backyard patio.

Design and Planning

Good stonework takes both physical and creative energy. It also takes the skills and procedures common to all successful projects: realistic expectations, reliable suppliers and subcontractors, good record keeping, patience, and an appreciation for sweat equity. At roughly 160 pounds to the cubic foot, stonework will test your mettle.

Landscaping with Stone can take the guesswork out of your project. Use the information to complete a project on your own, or rely on it for guidance when collaborating with a mason or designer.

The first four chapters help you think of stone as a landscaping element. Use them to guide you through defining the overall style of a project, evaluating the site, choosing the stone, and coordinating an installation. A chapter on tools and techniques will introduce you to some of the tools that could make your project go more smoothly. The plan presented in these chapters helps you stay organized, keep your momentum, and make the best use of your resources.

Stone Projects

Chapters 5 through 12 each look at a specific stonework project. These chapters feature the voices of experience—homeowners, designers, landscapers, and masons who generously contributed information for this book. Their projects are from geographic areas of the U.S. where natural stone is plentiful and there is a tradition of using stone in gardens and landscapes. Each chapter includes design information, dozens of photographs of stonework projects, and installation guidance.

Creating a water feature that looks as if it sprang from nature is easier than you might think.

▲ **This mortared fieldstone walkway** features a wood footbridge over a pond.

▶ **This wall made of native stones** is an ideal spot for a planter filled with colorful blooms.

WHY DO STONEWORK?

Each of us has our own reasons for choosing to participate in do-it-yourself projects. Financial incentives, the pleasure of physical work, the joy of learning, and creative stimulation are all familiar reasons to do-it-yourselfers. If you possess one or more of these inclinations, you can complete a landscaping project using stone. Technical and expressive abilities are important, but more than anything else, success hinges on your mental and physical investment in the project.

Use *Landscaping with Stone* to help you add natural beauty and value to your property. It is packed with the inspiration and technical know-how that will help you transform rough sketches and inspired daydreams into your own designs and completed stonework projects.

1

S tone may be the most versatile landscape building material available. Its qualities of strength and durability make it an excellent choice for garden paths, patios, and walls. But the decorative side of stone provides those landscape elements with a unique sense of style and makes stone a good choice for water features, rock gardens, and well-placed groupings that mimic nature or sculpture. This chapter will show you how to incorporate stone into your landscape design.

DESIGNING WITH STONE

Decide What You Like

▲ **This stone water feature** delights the senses.

▼ **Dry-laid patios** appear more informal than those with mortar-filled joints.

As you begin to plan your own project, you will need to make some decisions about the scope and elements in the project. What type of project are you planning? What are its proposed dimensions? What types of stone will you use for the project? Who will do the work?

Studying examples of existing stonework in walls, patios, and other landscape features is one of the best ways to begin to discover your preferences for stonework details. Stone found in nature, a neighbor's yard, the local botanical garden, and everything in between are places where you can see how stone is used. Not only can you learn what is possible from these examples, you can also discover what you like.

GATHERING INFORMATION FOR YOUR PROJECT

▌ Bring home samples from quarries or masonry supply yards.

▌ Mark examples in books and magazines that you like, both whole landscapes and specific elements.

▌ Take photos of constructed and natural landscapes, and stonework that appeal to you.

▌ Take measurements and make notes to go with photos: location, type of stone, contact person, and so on.

▌ Notice how different path materials feel underfoot and how they affect your walking pace.

▌ View the most appealing projects and natural settings in all seasons.

▌ View projects in the dark with artificial light if you'll use the area in the evening.

EXPLORE THE POSSIBILITIES

When trying to incorporate a new patio into your yard, add a rustic-looking stone wall to the garden, or build any stone-based project, rely on basic design principles to help the project best fit in with its surroundings.

SCALE AND PROPORTION. The scale and proportion of an object work hand in hand. The scale of something refers to its size as it relates to everything else. A 10-foot-high stone wall will tower over everything in the yard, including the people who use the space. It may be a good choice if you want total privacy and security, but a 3-foot-high wall may make more sense if you simply want to define an herb garden.

Proportion refers to the relationship of objects to one another based on size—the size of the patio is in proportion to the size of the yard. Good scale is achieved when all of the parts complement one another proportionally.

LINE. Simply put, lines define space, but they also suggest various qualities. A straight line implies strength and formality: a straight path almost always appears formal. A curving, winding path denotes a certain freedom and casualness.

BALANCE. In a landscape, balance refers to the effects created by the mix of elements you use. The features of a landscape are in balance when they look as though they belong together and the arrangement is pleasing to the eye. Balanced relationships can be either symmetrical or asymmetrical.

Remember that a stone patio will look its best when kept in proportion to the yard.

POPULAR STONEWORK PROJECTS

STONEWORK for gardens and landscapes generally fits into one of three categories: it imitates nature; it's functional; or it's sculptural. Some projects combine categories or serve multiple functions. Here are some additional stonework projects.

STONEWORK THAT IMITATES NATURE
- Ponds
- Streams and dry stream beds
- Waterfalls
- Rocky outcroppings
- Scree
- Boulders set in beds, open spaces, or woods
- Stepping-stones over water

FUNCTIONAL STONEWORK
- Stepping-stones
- Fire pits and fireplaces

- Pool surrounds and copings
- Erosion control
- Seating and tables
- Edgings
- Terraces
- Grade changes
- Lanterns
- Containers for plants
- Bridges

SCULPTURAL STONEWORK
- Specimen stones, one or a group
- Water bowls
- Birdbaths
- Carved or cast figurative and abstract pieces
- Relief carvings
- Mosaics
- Objects in stone or other materials incorporated into stonework

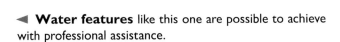 ◄ **Water features** like this one are possible to achieve with professional assistance.

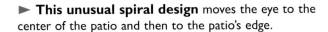 ► **This unusual spiral design** moves the eye to the center of the patio and then to the patio's edge.

HARMONY AND RHYTHM. In a harmonious plan, all of the elements share characteristics such as size, shape, or color. An example would be a patio and wall that are made from the same type stone. Rhythm refers to repeated patterns. When you vary one or more of the above traits in a repetitive pattern, it creates a visual rhythm. The key to creating good harmony and rhythm is balance.

TEXTURE AND COLOR. Stone is available in a variety of colors and textures. As you begin to design your project, you'll discover that stone can convey almost any feeling you want—grandeur, elegance, simplicity, solitude, durability, utility, and order are all possible. Stone can even suggest something other than what is. A dry streambed is a classic example of this.

DESIGN TIP

Find Inspiration Everywhere

Check garden and home decorating magazines for stonework ideas; ask to see the portfolios of designers or masons; and go on tours of local gardens. To find local garden tours, check with local garden clubs and the Garden Conservancy's Open Days Directory. (Visit www.gardenconservancy.org for more information.)

► **A colorful planted border** flanks a curving mortared staircase.

▼ **These well-placed boulders** look as though they have always been part of the site.

Aesthetic Decisions for Stonework

When you work with stone, you make decisions about the qualities of the stone you use, the quantities or distribution of the stone, and the way that the project transitions to its surroundings. For flat work such as patios and walkways, you also have to make choices about bedding—how the stone is set in place. The decisions you make about each of these factors will affect the overall look of your project and how well it is integrated into the site.

THE PHYSICAL QUALITIES OF STONE. The physical qualities of stone can contribute varying degrees of formality to a project. Variations in color and composition, the texture of exposed faces, fracture lines, and the size and shape of individual stones contribute to the distinctive character of each stone type.

Smooth surfaces are more formal that rough ones, large uniformly shaped pieces are more formal than irregular smaller pieces. For example, if you build a patio using 2-foot-square pieces of sawn bluestone set with -inch joints, it will be more formal or conservative than if you had used irregular shaped pieces of a stone with more varied color and with a rough or cleaved surface. (See "Choosing Between Formal and Informal Designs," pages 20–21.)

THE QUANTITY OR DISTRIBUTION OF STONE. Quantity or distribution refers to how much stone you use and how you arrange and space the stone. Distribution includes the relationship between stones in a grouping of stones, the ratio of stone to vegetation, and the way you combine different types of stone. In both walls and flat work, stones fitted tightly together create a more formal project than those with irregular or larger joints. In some projects, it's important to consider the amount of stone that will be hidden as vegetation matures. With foresight, you can create different effects by using seasonal changes. A hillside rock garden can be a riot of cultivated color in summer, for example, but can change to a wild, rugged place in winter.

Distribution is perhaps most critical when you make an artful arrangement of large stones. The stones must be close enough together to create a composition but be far enough apart that each makes a distinct contribution to the overall arrangement.

TRANSITIONS. It can be challenging to figure out how to transition from your stonework to the surrounding area, such as to lawn or a driveway. Fortunately there are many options from which to choose. If you're not sure what will work best, try experimenting with different treatments in a small area to evaluate possible solutions. Ground covers, timbers, bark mulch, gravel, a grade change, and hedging are common transitioning solutions. You can even plant one or more shrubs to hide a difficult transition for which you can't find another solution. Transitions around a patio are relatively easy and straightforward. Fencing, flowerbeds, hedging, or a stone wall are all commonly used.

It's easy and tempting to ignore transitions until after the main elements of a project are installed. Don't! Careless transitions detract from your project and may forever look like an afterthought. Some examples of these careless transitions include abrupt drop-offs from patios to lawns or a wall that ends in the landscape without relating to another landscape element.

▲ **Both dry-laid** and mortared stone walls rely on staggered joints for stability.

▼ **Plant retaining walls** with hardy plants to create vertical rock gardens.

BEDDING CHOICES. Stone is either dry laid or mortared in place. With either option, bedding variables affect the appearance of the stonework. Variables include the size of the joints, or spaces between stones, whether the spaces are filled in, and the fill material. As a general rule, mortared, uniform, narrow joints are the most formal. Going back to the patio example, if your joints are irregular and large enough for planting a ground cover, the effect will be more casual than if the joints are uniform and filled with sand. Again, experiment with different possibilities. Notice the choices that designers have made in similar projects. Observations like these help inform your decisions.

SMART TIP

Don't Forget about Future Maintenance
When making decisions about bedding for flat work, think about maintenance. Mortared joints require the least amount of maintenance, though they do eventually crumble. Sand-filled joints need to be refilled periodically. Planted and sand-filled joints require occasional weeding from blown-in seed.

Expert craftspeople can create designs such as this outdoor patio seating area constructed from native stone.

1

DESIGNING WITH STONE

CHOOSING BETWEEN FORMAL AND INFORMAL DESIGNS

THE TYPE OF STONE YOU SELECT and its distribution, transitions, and bedding will influence the look and formality of your project. Here are some elements to consider.

FORMAL DESIGNS

- smooth surface
- cut or sawn stone
- uniform, rectangular shapes
- repetitive pattern
- uniform color
- homogeneous composition
- small joints
- uniform joints
- mortared joints
- one type of stone
- tall retainer walls
- uniform size and color of gravel
- large project (big patio, large water feature)

EDGING MATERIALS
- square timbers
- brick or other uniformly shaped stones
- gravel
- formal flower beds

INFORMAL DESIGNS

- rough or irregular surface
- cleaved or weathered flat surface
- irregular shapes
- random or multiple patterns
- variations in color
- nonhomogeneous composition
- large joints (¾ in. or more)
- irregular joint width
- sand, gravel, soil with ground cover in joints
- two or more types of stone
- terraced retainer walls
- mixed gravel
- small-scale projects

EDGING MATERIALS

- round timbers
- random-size stones
- bark mulch
- ground covers

1

DESIGNING WITH STONE

DEVELOPING A DESIGN DIRECTION

Have you collected numerous photos of stonework constructed with a particular kind of stone or pattern? Perhaps a particular color, texture, or shape of stone dominates your samples. It's a good indication that you're forming personal preferences about stonework when these decision-making patterns emerge.

Notice what is most outstanding about the projects you like. Sometimes it's not even the stone, but something adjacent to it, such as water or a specimen plant. Specific rather than general observations yield the most information and build confidence for your decisions about these details. Asking questions about existing projects helps you identify overlooked considerations, too.

Often ideas and features that continue to engage you end up influencing the look of your project. Or you may deliberately incorporate specific ideas or features you've discovered.

Another indicator of emerging preferences is your intuitive response to a type of stone or installation. Sometimes this is called comfort level. Whatever you call it, the experience is an overriding sense that the stone, pattern, type of installation, and so on, is right for you, right for the site, or would just work well.

ANALYZE YOUR RESEARCH

AS YOU LOOK AT completed stonework projects and natural landscapes that you like, ask the following:

▌ What do I like about the stone?

▌ How is the transition made from the stone to whatever adjoins or abuts it?

▌ Can I identify specific features or elements besides the stone that make this space pleasing to me?

▌ How do the shape, arrangement, texture, quantity, and types of stone contribute to the overall formality and effect?

▌ How would I describe the overall effect?

▌ How do I respond to the quality of "fullness" or "emptiness" in this installation?

▌ Does the stonework define or create space?

▌ Does the stonework create a microclimate by trapping heat or creating shade?

▌ How much stone is used?

▌ In the settings that you like the best, what percentage of the total project area is stone?

▌ How much stone is visible at different times of the year, i.e., with or without plants in leaf?

◀ **In this sunny spot,** stepping-stones complement rather than overwhelm the plantings in the area.

▶ **In many areas,** native stone is the material of choice for outdoor living areas.

▼ **This view** shows what you can do when combining different materials in one design.

TRADEOFFS. Ultimately, there are tradeoffs between design goals, site possibilities, and the budget. Many homeowners find this part of the design process the hardest. In these cases, it is often best to seek out the opinions of friends and acquaintances. Eventually, you start to trust in the process, and an aesthetic emerges that works for you and the site.

INSPIRATION FROM THE SITE

The site for your project is a valuable source of inspiration. Often the land itself suggests use and design possibilities that can influence the overall project plan. Professional designers always consider a site's assets as part of the design phase of a project; this approach makes sense for homeowners as well. It's usually less expensive to work with, rather than alter, existing site conditions. It's also easier—and you're more likely—to end up with a project that is well integrated into its surroundings. You'll find more on working with the site in Chapter 2.

USE PROPS

Visual aids help you explore ideas and prepare for installing your project. Use cardboard cutouts to make path "stones" a pattern for a patio, or as a way to envision a retainer wall or steps. Use malleable materials such as chicken wire and crumpled-up paper to test the location of

large boulders. Branches and small trees can represent future mature plants. Garden hose and rope work well to outline paths, beds, water features, or a patio. Even grade stakes and string are useful to help you visualize the space as you plan to reconfigure it.

BE CURIOUS ABOUT YOUR MATERIALS. Play with stone the way an artist experiments with materials. Explore and test patterns, spacing, and the effect of light and shade. Observe how different stones look and feel when they are wet. Study the relationship between stone and its surroundings in existing projects. These exercises provide a basis for decisions that will affect the look of your stonework.

Nature is your best teacher for stone projects that mimic natural features. If you plan a project such as a streambed or rocky wooded hillside, studying the way stone is naturally distributed in these settings can help you adapt desirable qualities to your site.

It takes effort to adapt your personal style to stonework. A spirit of adventure helps, too. But if you explore possibilities early on in a project, you'll find it easier to make design decisions. What you learn during the exploration process makes it possible to turn a pile of stone into something that pleases you.

Although the designer combined brick with stone, the walls, borders, steps, and walkway work well together.

1

DESIGNING WITH STONE

WALKWAYS & STEPS

IN PURELY FUNCTIONAL TERMS, steps, paths, walkways, and stepping-stones help you get from one part of the yard to another. But they also serve as a unifying element in the landscape design by providing your eye with a bridge that connects one design element or area with another. You can strengthen this connection by using walkways or steps to connect elements, such as two stone walls or a wall and patio, that are made from the same type stone. Tie the whole design together by using a similar stone for the walkway.

▲ **This well-built wall** and stairway defines the boundaries of the patio area.

◄ **Slabs of cut stone** serve as steps that wind up a steep incline.

▼ **Native stone** easily blends with the surrounding area.

1

DESIGNING WITH STONE

MORE WALKWAYS & STEPS

◄ **The gentle curve** of these wood and gravel steps adds interest to the landscape.

► **The random pattern** of this walkway creates an informal feeling for the area.

▼ **When placing** large stone slabs, strive for a natural arrangement, such as the one shown here.

Don't be afraid to juxtapose shapes and patterns to create a truly unique design. The mixed-media pathway here includes linear cut stones, scalloped precast concrete with gravel infill, and flagstone surrounding the wooden posts.

STONE PATIOS

PATIOS ADD THE NATURAL STRUCTURE found indoors to outdoor living spaces. They are destinations that people in the yard seek out and tend to gravitate toward. As with any interior living space, design patios so that they can accommodate any activities you plan for the area. Most people plan patios as spaces that allow them to sit and enjoy the scenery, but don't forget other possible uses, including areas to entertain, cooking spaces, and places that allow you to keep an eye on young children who want to play outside.

◄ **The inlaid design** on this stone patio gives it a personalized touch.

► **A well-sited patio** incorporates the natural scenery into one's backyard.

► **Stone complements other materials,** such as the weathered shingles, outdoor furniture, and the natural plantings shown here.

 # WALLS

WALLS FORM BOUNDARIES that separate your yard from your neighbor's or divide up your property into smaller sections. A stone retaining wall or a group of walls turns a sloping yard into level, usable areas. Stone walls also provide a feeling of stability and strength that few other landscape elements can. Stone walls are either dry laid or mortared in place. A dry-laid wall tends to be more casual than a mortared version, but the selection of stone and the design of the wall determine the look of the finished project.

▶ **Using natural materials, like regional stacking stone,** always helps a design blend in with the surrounding area.

▼ **Create dry-laid retaining walls** with field stones from your property.

▲ **Using similar dressed stones** of varied size and shape leads to a pleasing overall design. "Dressed" stones are stones that appear to be intentionally shaped.

◄ **A mortared fieldstone wall** (see page 195) serves as a foundation for flowering plants.

▼ **The sizes and shapes** of these stones contribute to the informal look of this dry-laid wall.

MORE WALLS

Dry-laid fieldstone walls impart a feeling of solidity to a landscape.

▲ **When researching** stone projects, look for examples where the stone complements the surroundings.

▼ **While most stone walls** run straight, the occasional curve adds design interest.

▲ **Mortared walls** may be challenging to build, but they make unusual designs possible.

▼ **A solid-looking stone wall** appears to support the building constructed above it.

STONE FEATURES

A STONE FEATURE can be a rock garden, a grouping of stones that has the look of sculpture, a birdbath, dry creek bed, or any one of dozens of other designs. In fact, most large water features rely on stone to provide the borders for the feature, and in streams and waterfalls, stone often directs water flow. You can let your imagination and creativity run a little wild when designing a stone feature, but you must still take care in placing the stones and arranging them in a way that makes good design sense.

◀ **A circular stone patio** is the perfect location for a fire pit.

▼ **There is an art** to placing very large stones in a landscape (see Design Tip on the opposite page).

DESIGN TIP

Stone As a Design Element

You can use stone to change the look and feel of a space. The size and shape of the stones, their color, quantity, spacing, and placement all contribute to the overall character of your project. Note these elements as you look at examples of stonework.

Some ways to do this are deciding which side of stone is the good side and from which angle it would best be viewed. For a sense of permanence, plant rocks by partially burying them. It also works well to group rocks of various sizes to create a focal point or landscape accent with a sense of balance.

▶ **This water feature** looks almost too natural to have been built.

▼ **River-washed stones** complete a bubbling spring.

MORE STONE FEATURES

► **The designer** used shards of stone to create this elegant garden urn.

▼ **This dramatic water feature** is mostly made of steel for the waterfall and spillway areas, and is flanked by a thin stack stone wall wrapped in steel mesh. The mesh can be used as a climbing plant support if desired. Purpose-built kit components to your DIY plan will be helpful.

▲ **This unusual landscape** includes two sculptures around which the space was designed. Focal elements include the built-in bench with three circular windows, the tile sculputre on a layer of polished stone, and the bubbling fountain with concrete surrounding. The dry-stacked stone wall is used to tie the seemingly unrelated elements together into a unified garden space.

▶ **Stone gives a site authenticity,** and it helps hide the edges of a pond liner.

▼ **This cute fellow** stands guard over the strawberry patch.

2

Once you have a picture in your mind of the stonework project you want, it's time to take a long, hard look at the building site. You can make the best use of your site only when you have a thorough understanding of its limitations as well as its assets. Having a detailed overview or "big picture" is key to refining your project design. No detail is too small to be ignored when you are planning a stonework project—it's far easier to correct an error with your pencil than with your back.

PLANNING YOUR
PROJECT

SITE EVALUATION CHECKLIST

USE THIS LIST to evaluate the site of the project. If a contractor or landscaping firm is doing the work, use this list to check its work.

LOCATE
- Property lines
- Rights-of-way (Check the property deed.)
- Buried services (Maps are available from utility companies.)
- Telecom cables
- Water, gas, sewer, and electric lines
- Drainage tile (Check with previous owner or the architect, or look for outlets in low spots.)

IDENTIFY
- Soil type(s)
- New permanent paths for foot and vehicle traffic
- Topography to preserve or alter
- Vegetation to preserve and store for reinstallation
- Vegetation to protect from damage during installation
- Vulnerable roots of large trees and plants
- Microclimate possibilities
- Water to incorporate into plan or divert
- Stone to incorporate into plan or remove
- New drainage requirements
- Areas to light artificially and the kind of light desired
- Airflow patterns to maintain or alter
- Sun and shade to maintain or alter
- Points of transition from existing to new features
- Impact of new features on possible future building or landscaping plans

ZONING RESTRICTIONS AND PERMIT REQUIREMENTS (Check with municipal offices.)
- Setback requirements
- Permits
- Erosion control (large projects)

SITE MANAGEMENT REQUIREMENTS
- Access for deliveries
- Physical space to unload
- Adequate ground conditions to support loaded vehicles
- Travel paths for construction-related activities
- Storage space for stone, base or bedding material; excavated topsoil and subsoil; plants
- Boundary of excavated area
- Off-site disposal of excess excavated soil
- Space to maneuver equipment
- Flags or ropes to delineate unsafe areas

FOR WORK WITH MORTAR
- Access to water
- Disposal of cleanup wastewater
- Waterproof storage for cement

INSURANCE
- Homeowner's policy with existing coverage and options to obtain additional coverage for construction
- Certificates of insurance from subcontractors

Even adding a small backyard patio requires that you check for buried utilities.

Defining the Site

When creating a stonework project, the space you'll need always extends beyond its footprint. The site will include access areas for deliveries; storage areas for stone, backfill, or bedding material; storage for disturbed subsoil and topsoil that will be redistributed afterwards; a place to care for plants; underground utilities and drainage pipes; and buildings or parts of buildings that are essentially part of the site. For example, if you install a patio adjacent to one side of the house, that side of the house is part of the site, along with any windows, porches, or decks that offer views of the site.

Your site may also include locations for temporary dikes or ditches that prevent erosion during the installation. If your project involves the use of large equipment, the space needed to maneuver the equipment is also part of your site.

BE NEIGHBORLY. Sometimes a site limited to one property isn't big enough to manage a project efficiently. If this is your situation, consider asking an adjoining property owner for permission to use whatever additional space you need to handle materials efficiently. It may be a good idea to draw up a written agreement with the neighbor. Or look into using part of the street if possible.

SITE EVALUATION

Unlike the mental free rein you give yourself when exploring aesthetic choices, you need to be more deliberate with the site evaluation. It is literally an inventory of the items on your property. No detail is too small to ignore: identify all of the site's features, potential, and limits. Then transfer this information to plan and elevation drawings.

No detail is too small to ignore during a site evaluation, especially when you are planning an elaborate water feature.

2

PLANNING YOUR PROJECT

BECOME A SOIL SLEUTH

The quality of the soil is the most critical existing condition for the long-term stability of your stonework. It's especially important to know its history if you want to build a large project. Tall walls and retainer walls need adequate and properly compacted fill. Without it, the stonework will sag or creep and eventually fall apart.

Test holes are sometimes enough to determine the presence of fill and other characteristics of the soil. Soil that digs easily is likely to be either uncompacted fill or too sandy to safely support large stonework. Undisturbed gravelly soils are ideal. They require the least amount of base, backfill material, and supplemental drainage. Any other soil type is likely to require additional excavation and replacement with more stable material.

If your soil drains poorly, you may need to divert water by creating a swale or installing a French drain (also called drainage tile).

This is also the time to evaluate storm runoff patterns. Consider how your project may change the direction or volume of runoff. Include construction details and landscape features that will improve rainwater infiltration and prevent erosion or flooding that could arise after the project is complete.

MINIMIZE EXCAVATION SURPRISES. Before you begin to excavate, explore your site. Check for large rocks, ledge, and unusual fill in the areas you want to excavate or reshape. Believe it or not, it's possible to find such things as old sidewalk curbing buried a foot under a suburban lawn.

To check an area, drive an iron bar to the estimated excavation depth every 3 to 4 feet in the entire area. Wherever possible, modify your design to work with existing large rocks and ledge. It's expensive to blast and move massive rocks—especially when uncovering them can instead reveal a landscaping treasure.

EROSION. In stonework, erosion concerns usually aren't about soil loss, but there is concern that a heavy rain will collapse a bank, leaving you with a muddy mess. Preventive measures can minimize or eliminate erosion problems. For small- to moderate-sized projects, dig ditches and place hay-bale dikes to redirect water. Cover exposed soil, including piles of soil for backfilling or grading, with landscape fabric or plastic. To temporarily protect dry soil from wind erosion, lay weed barrier fabric over the exposed soil and anchor it with rocks, soil, concrete blocks, or wood.

For an interesting design variation, create a double landscape border using river stones and gravel.

CONSTRUCTION TIP

Estimating Time

If you need to estimate how long it will take to install your project, ask a mason how long it would take an experienced person to complete each of the project steps. Depending on your skill level, add anywhere from 100 to 200 percent of the time that the mason estimates. Or use the technique of estimating time as best you can and then doubling that figure.

DEVELOPING A SITE PLAN

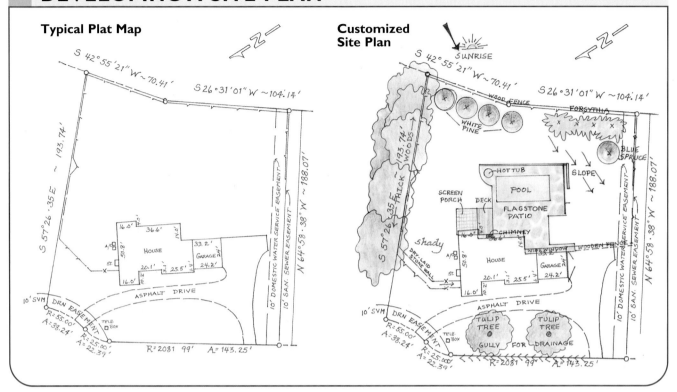

Typical Plat Map

Customized Site Plan

CREATE SITE DRAWINGS

Drawings help you plan, solve problems, test ideas, communicate, and organize your site management activities. Their necessity and usefulness depends on the size of the project, your work style, and your ability. People with extraordinary spatial abilities can build complex constructions—even entire buildings—without a single drawing. The rest of us, though, need drawings to keep the details of the project straight and the project organized.

SIMPLE PLANS. For straightforward uncomplicated projects, use field notes and sketches from the site evaluation to create a set of plan and elevation drawings. Your plan drawing includes fixed points such as specimen plants, buildings, and utility lines as well as the project footprint and any anticipated new drainage lines. On the elevation drawing indicate features such as grade changes, depth of buried utilities, and anticipated excavation and fill requirements.

For projects with complicated grade changes, you may want to use plan and elevation overlays on your "existing conditions" drawings. These can help you anticipate troublesome transitions or space constraints.

A pleasingly random configuration of flagstone slabs leads to the more formal stone entryway of this home.

HOW MUCH IS ENOUGH? A master plan for high-use areas, excavation and grading plans, construction details, and planting plans reduce errors and help you visualize the process and the finished project. The number of drawings you make and the details you include are a matter of personal preference.

Your plans can't be too accurate. Check measurements a few days after you record them or, even better, have

Large and small stones found on site can become a beautifully natural part of the overall landscape design.

someone else check them. Make it a habit to double-check measurements throughout a project. If you have more than one set of drawings, it's important to note changes on all copies. To avoid confusion, date the drawings whenever you make changes.

BE A GOOD NEIGHBOR

ACCIDENTS HAPPEN so it is a good idea to anticipate how a borrowed access or storage area might be damaged. For example, excavation equipment can tear up lawn; a load of boulders dumped on the road can damage blacktop; and dense materials such as crushed stone, soil, or plants will kill underlying vegetation in as little as a week. Avoid problems by making a written agreement for the use of a neighbor's—or the town's—property. A municipality may have a form and process for such agreements, but you'll need to draft one for a neighbor.

The agreement should include:

▮ Start and completion dates
▮ Description of the area, including pictures from several angles prior to using it
▮ Description of how you plan on using the property
▮ A clause to restore the land to its former condition. Check with your insurance company ahead of time so that you can answer liability insurance questions.

MANAGING THE WORK SITE

Site management refers to organizing all the details that determine whether or not a project can proceed efficiently and safely. Imagine discovering halfway through a project that you must move several tons of stone because it's preventing access to a part of the work area. Similarly, it's pretty frustrating to realize that you could use a backhoe—instead of a wheelbarrow—to move backfill if you'd only put the piles in a different spot.

To avoid scenarios like this, walk through the steps of your project on the plan drawings and on the site itself. Use a tape measure and flagging ribbon to lay out features and mark critical locations, and talk to the delivery driver, mason, and anyone else who will need access. An equipment operator's criteria for safe, adequate working conditions may not be the same as yours. Steep terrain, water, mud, and unknowns about buried utilities can easily turn into delays.

USE YOUR DRAWING. If your site is complicated, use a copy of your plan drawing to indicate, in scale, storage and delivery areas and where equipment can maneuver. Better yet, use marking paint to designate these areas on the site. If you're working in a confined space, the difference between a pile of stone taking up a 10 x 10-foot area or 20 x 20-foot area could be critical.

CONSTRUCTION TIP

Make Organizing Easy

Make two lists for your project. On one, list the parts or steps of the project; on the other, list the purchases and contracted services. Combine the two lists in the order you need to act on them. Do this, and you will have completed a large part of your work plan. To organize large or complex projects, plot the parts of the project and purchases on a timeline.

PROFESSIONAL EXPERTISE

If you are handling the design and management phases of a large project yourself, have a professional assess your plans. Many landscape designers, though they may not have the academic training of a landscape architect, are equally knowledgeable about stonework. The expertise of masons and landscape contractors usually lies in installation rather than design; however, many of them have the project management and design skills needed to review plans for a project. In general, you're looking for the opinion of someone with significant experience in the type of stone project you are planning.

2

PLANNING YOUR PROJECT

The mundane work of site evaluation leads to beautiful results, such as this brightly colored garden.

FINDING A PRO. Locate professionals through word-of-mouth recommendations, direct contact with individuals whose work you have seen and liked, or you can ask at a garden center or stone supplier for recommendations. Although it may take time, be as diligent in finding someone to advise you as you would be in hiring him or her to do the actual work. Examine his or her portfolio; ask for and check references. Meet with the professionals to discuss your project. You can expect to pay between $35 and $100 an hour for a professional review of your plans.

FINAL CHECKS. With your site plan in hand, mentally walk through the steps of the project as you physically walk the site. A walk-through is a good way to catch overlooked parts of a project or forgotten purchases.

Mark critical locations with grade stakes and flagging ribbon, spray paint, or weather-resistant markers; it can be difficult to find these locations once you alter the terrain. If a project will take several months or longer, keep a keyed map with measurements taken from fixed points. Take photos to create a record for future renovations and as documentation if you sell the property.

THE BUDGET AS A PLANNING AID

Even though you might not think of it this way, a budget is a useful planning aid. Because you develop it as you create the plan, the budget often contains the most comprehensive list of materials and services that you'll need for the project. One planning strategy is to work from a detailed budget to create your work plan. Conversely, a good budget can serve as a cross-reference to anything you might have overlooked while planning your project. No matter how you use the project budget beyond its cost-accounting function, you'll find that the more detailed you make it, the more useful it is.

HOW MUCH WILL IT COST?

When you put cost figures to a project, it culminates the planning phase and sets the installation process in motion. If you are your own general contractor, many businesses will give you a contractor's price and an account for theduration of your project. Prices for construction materials fluctuate, and some suppliers will guarantee you a price if you make the purchase within a given period of time. Insist on written estimates or bids from designers, contractors, and subcontractors for any work they perform. Agree on the terms for payment beforehand. Use the budget categories in "Typical Budget Categories," opposite page, to help you finalize your project budget.

This oversized water feature filled with river rock and surrounded by native plants creates a simple, serene focal point in this garden.

Large stones, such as these, must be delivered to the site by heavy equipment.

TYPICAL BUDGET CATEGORIES

BUDGETS have a way of clarifying goals like nothing else can. Use these general categories to help finalize your project budget. Few projects include all of the categories listed here; choose the ones that apply to your project. If you purchase materials six months or more after drawing up the budget, increase estimated costs or the contingency category by 10 percent.

BUDGET CATEGORIES
- Permits
- Removal of existing plants to hold for replanting or disposal
- Removal of excess sod and soil
- Care of plants during construction
- Stone by cubic yards or square feet
- Specimen stones
- Base and/or backfill crushed rock or sand in cubic yards
- Other project materials
- Equipment rental
- Tool purchases
- Sales taxes
- Drainage changes
- Erosion control
- Trucking or other costs to get stone on site
- Temporary protection of work area
- Temporary roadway or access
- New or relocated water, electrical, or telecom lines
- Cleanup costs
- Disposal of excess stone
- Site remediation
- Design fees
- Contractor and subcontractor fees for earth-moving, moving stone, and related landscaping
- Consultation, contracted design, or installation services
- Insurance
- Change in property tax (Ask an assessor how landscaping improvements are valued.)
- Contingencies—a minimum 20 percent of the total project budget

2

PLANNING YOUR PROJECT

3

The stone for your project can come from any number of sources, including quarries and garden centers. But don't overlook other sources, such as your own backyard, the fields near your home, and demolition or blasting sites. In many of those areas, the stone is free. Due to obvious shipping and storage problems, most stone is quarried and sold locally, although special orders are possible. A quick online search will list local stone suppliers.

STONE AS A BUILDING MATERIAL

From the garden center to a local spot nearby, stones can be found all over to create a variety of enchanting structures.

Stone Classifications

Masons and builders describe stone in different ways, depending on the context. You'll find it classified by its geological type, trade names, or the dimensions or shapes commonly used in construction and landscaping. For example, granite is a trade name for a specific type of igneous rock—the geologic classification. For landscaping, granite is sold as pavers, blocks or ashlar, steps, specimen stones, rubble, and crushed rock in a variety of sizes. Go to a quarry or stone yard, and you will see examples of stone that are cut in uniform shapes with smooth surfaces, called dressed stone, and the same stone in a more natural, unfinished state, called rough. (See "Terms for Stone," opposite.)

TERMS FOR STONE

THE FOLLOWING ARE COMMON WORDS used in the landscaping trade to describe different types of stone. Find more definitions for specific stones and stone products on pages 58–63. You may also find other words used that are specific to a geographic region. Visit a stoneyard to learn about the types of stone available to you.

COBBLESTONE   Small rounded stone used for paving. Also, any small-dimension milled stone that is used for paving.

CUT STONE   Any stone that has been milled or worked by hand to a specific shape or dimension.

CRUSHED ROCK   Small-dimension material available in a range of colors and sizes with either a smooth or angular surface.

DRESSED STONE   Usually quarried stone that has been squared off on all sides and has a smooth face.

FACE   The exposed side of a stone.

FIELDSTONE   Stone as it is found in the natural environment.

FLAGGING   Paving for walks or patios made from flagstone.

PAVERS   Any stone milled to a uniform size and shape, typically about the size of a brick, and used to surface walkways and patios.

QUARRY DRESSED   A term for stone that is squared off on all sides but has a rough face. Sometimes called semidressed stone.

ROUGH STONE   Stone as it comes from the quarry.

RUBBLE   Stone blasted on a construction site or pieces left over from cutting quarried stone. Also, any low-grade stone used for fill in a stone wall.

SEMIDRESSED   A term for stone that is squared off on two or more sides but has a rough face.

SPECIMEN STONE   A stone with unusual color, surface, or form that is used alone or in an arrangement of other speciman stones for its sculptural or decorative qualities.

STONE NAMES. The composition of geological stone types varies widely from one place to another, as do the trade names given to each type of stone. The geological classification is sometimes used as a trade name, or a quarry may make up a trade name. Wilmington Schist refers to a specific type of metamorphic rock quarried in southern Vermont. It also happens to be a trade name.

Moss rock is a common name for a type of stone found in southern and central New Mexico. Although the name does not really convey any information about the stone, New Mexico masons know it as a locally quarried type of sandstone. However, someone could make pavers out of moss rock, and market them under the trade name "South Sun Pavers." Sometimes a photograph or a visual inspection is the only way to accurately identify the stone type.

EVALUATING STONE

When selecting stone for a project, you need to determine whether the type of stone would be appropriate for the planned use and whether the stone type itself is fairly uniform or extremely variable.

Determining whether a stone is appropriate is a straightforward matter of looking at its aesthetic and structural characteristics. Aesthetic characteristics such as color, texture, size, and shape contribute to the overall look of your project. If color uniformity is important, select a type of stone that can be reliably tooled or shaped without revealing other colors. Structural characteristics are critical for ease of construction and the durability of the installation. You may need to consider porosity, mechanical strength, quality of building surfaces, and how easy it is to cut, split, or shape the stone.

▲ **When ordering stone,** it is best to bring photos and samples of the stone you want to the stone yard.

▼ **For projects** such as a long path, ask the delivery driver to space the pallets along the length of the project.

▲ **Visit projects** you admire to learn how to put the natural variations of stone to good use in your project.

◄ **Before starting any project,** especially a complicated one such as this, experiment with the stone first.

VARIATIONS IN STONE. Stone is never homogeneous; there can be variations in quality even among different stones from the same quarry. It takes vigilance, visual inspection, and an occasional whack of a hammer to evaluate the quality of a specific type of stone. If you can personally select the stone for your project, do it.

Some stone can appear to be good building stone but begin to crumble within a few years. Be cautious if stone seems under priced. And ask the supplier for the names of masons who use it. Take the time to call and ask the masons about their experience with the stone.

If you are unsure about the suitability of a local stone, you can sometimes find information about it through the Extension Service or a U.S. Soil Conservation office. Masons, designers, and landscape architects who use natural stone are often familiar with the qualities of stone common to an area.

3 STONE AS A BUILDING MATERIAL

SMALL-DIMENSION MATERIALS

Small-dimension materials such as gravel, crushed rock, pea stone, and bedding sand are sometimes unavailable from building stone suppliers. Visit sand and gravel yards to become familiar with the colors, sizes, and surface qualities of those that are available. Take pictures or bring along sturdy sacks or crates to take samples home.

Gravel is an excellent base for many stone projects because it provides stability and creates good drainage. Ask your supplier about the availability of gravel that packs and drains well. Each quarry uses different names for its gravel and stone products. Keep a written record for comparison shopping and ordering.

NATURAL STONE VS. FABRICATED STONE

For applications like decorative home cladding or an outdoor kitchen island exterior, stone veneer makes a durable, lightweight, easy-to-use, and relatively inexpensive alternative to constructing natural stone walls. Veneer is essentially a stone skin that acts more like siding and less like a structural wall. Inch-thick veneer blocks adhere to a vertical mortar bed like wallpaper on adhesive. It offers the timeless appearance of a stone wall but skips the footer and ninety percent of the physical stone itself.

Collect samples of small stones so that you can experiment with combining colors and textures.

When it comes to stone veneer choices, they fall into two basic categories: natural stone and manufactured (or fabricated) stone. (See "Stone Products for Landscaping," pages 58–63.) Natural stone veneer is made by slicing inch-thick faces from quarried stone blocks. It offers all the imperfections, subtle color variations, and texture details that make each individual piece unique. Fabricated stone is essentially molded concrete that is colored and textured to give the impression of natural stone; although each design includes multiple unique molds, this option delivers a highly uniform appearance. Fabricated stone also weighs about twenty percent less than natural stone.

While natural stone is heavier and costs slightly more than fabricated stone, it is more durable and will not fade with age. Fabricated stone, on the other hand, is easier for do-it-yourselfers to handle and can be installed on some substrates where natural stone cannot, such as drywall.

THE COST OF STONE

FACTORS that affect the price of stone include

▌ Type of stone
▌ Building qualities
▌ Point of origin
▌ Delivery charges

PRICE, AVAILABILITY & QUANTITY

All other things being equal, the more dressed stone is, the higher the price. For paving, large, uniformly shaped pieces are typically more expensive than smaller or randomly shaped pieces of the same type and quality.

Because so much stone sold for landscaping is available in more than one form, ask a supplier or quarry if it is available as a special order if you don't find what you want. Almost all commercially available stone is sold by the cubic yard, either loose or by the pallet. Specimen stones may be priced individually without regard to measurements.

HOW MUCH DO YOU NEED? To figure out how much stone you need, first calculate the cubic volume of stone for the project. Then add a percentage for waste. The amount of extra stone you need to order depends on the type of stone and the application. You don't have waste with specimen stones of course, and you can minimize waste for sand and gravel with good calculations. Brick and other small uniform materials have as little as 5 percent waste. If you build with natural fieldstone, you may order up to 50 percent extra. How much you'll need depends on the quality of the stone, what you are building, the look you want, and how much time you are willing to spend on shaping stones to fit.

Try to get a second opinion when you are deciding how much stone to order. An informed opinion can minimize both shortages and overages, as well as save you problems with disposing of extra material. The supplier or a mason familiar with the stone and the application can help you calculate accurately.

CONSTRUCTION TIP

Using Leftover Stone

If you are building a stone wall, use waste stone to fill the space between two wythes, or it can be used as fill behind a retainer wall. Smaller dimension leftover stone can also be put to good use for narrow maintenance paths through garden areas.

Combine stone with a variety of plants that bloom in different seasons to create an ever-changing landscape.

STONE PRODUCTS FOR LANDSCAPING

The landscaping projects found in this book require a variety of materials that may be unfamiliar to some readers. This is a quick reference to many of the products you may need for a stone project. It is important to note that some of these materials may be sold under other names because of branding or regional vernacular.

#57 STONE

Gray or tan clean, screened, angular gravel. Individual rocks range in size from $\frac{1}{2}$ to $1\frac{1}{2}$ inches.

▮ **Uses:** Retaining wall backfill material, French drains, driveway surfaces

▮ **Sold by:** Cubic yard

#78 STONE AND #89 STONE

Gray or tan washed, angular gravel. #78 stone averages $\frac{3}{8}$ to $\frac{1}{2}$ inch, while #89 stone is slightly smaller from $\frac{3}{32}$ to $\frac{3}{8}$ inch.

▮ **Uses:** Walkway and driveway surfaces

▮ **Sold by:** Cubic yard

ASHLAR

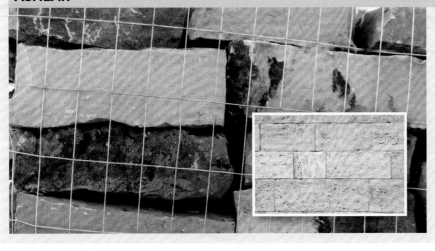

Any stone that has been individually worked until squared into a rectangle or cube. Ashlar tends to yield tighter joints and less waste because of the highly consistent shape. This consistency also makes it faster and easier to lay than undressed stone.

▮ **Uses:** Walls and buildings

▮ **Sold by:** Ton or pallet

BELGIAN BLOCK

Large square or rectangular blocks of quarried stone, usually about the size of a large brick. Fairly smooth on all faces and slightly rounded at the corners.

▌**Uses:** Edging for driveways, gardens, and pathways, paving material for driveways and walls

▌**Sold by:** Ton or pallet

CRUSHER RUN

Unscreened #57 stone includes all particle sizes from 1½ inch and smaller. Drains well when compacted.

▌**Uses:** Stable base material for patios, walkways, and retaining walls

▌**Sold by:** Cubic yard

FLAGSTONE

General name for many types of flat, thin sedimentary stone. Flagstone typically has a 1 to 2 inch thickness. A wide range of colors and color patterns are available. Flagstone may be used with its rough natural edge or can be shaped.

▌**Uses:** Paving material for patios and walkways, capstone for walls, roofing

▌**Sold by:** Ton, pallet, or square foot

3

STONE AS A BUILDING MATERIAL

LAVA ROCK

Lightweight, porous, gravel-like rock formed from a volcanic eruption, typically reddish brown, gray, or black. Average individual rock size is 1½ to 2 inches.

▮ **Uses:** Mulch, groundcover, gas firepit substrate

▮ **Sold by:** Cubic yard

MANUFACTURED STONE

A manufactured concrete veneer material that is molded and colored to look like natural stone. It is lighter weight than natural stone veneer and some pigments fade over time.

▮ **Uses:** Wall cladding, fireplace surrounds, decorative interior applications

▮ **Sold by:** T Square foot, linear foot (for corner pieces), or by the piece

MARBLE CHIPS

White, clean, angular gravel, screened to different size categories, typically smaller than 1½ inches. Marble chips can raise the pH of underlying soil.

▮ **Uses:** Pathway surface, mulch

▮ **Sold by:** Cubic yard

NATURAL STONE VENEER

Slices of natural stone that are cut from pieces of quarried stone. Natural stone veneer goes on like wallpaper, adhering to a vertical mortar bed. It does not require basal support like a traditional stone wall. Details like naturally occurring imperfections and subtle variations in texture and color are the hallmark of natural stone veneer.

▍**Uses:** Wall cladding, fireplace surrounds, and interior applications (e.g., shower surrounds and kitchen backsplashes)

▍**Sold by:** Square foot, linear foot (for corner pieces), or by the piece

PEA GRAVEL

Small, rounded, smooth stones that have been screened to size. Available in different sizes from different suppliers, with common sizes ranging between $3/32$ and $1/2$ inch.

▍**Uses:** Durable surface for walkways, playgrounds, patios, and other high-traffic areas

▍**Sold by:** Cubic yard

RIVER ROCK

Gray, tan, white, and brown smooth, rounded stones. Sorted or screened to different size categories as large as 10 inches.

▍**Uses:** Walking surfaces, water features, dry stream beds, mulch, edging

▍**Sold by:** Cubic yard

3

STONE AS A BUILDING MATERIAL

SAND

Granular material of fine mineral particles. The best type of sand for stonework is concrete sand, which is screened and washed for a coarse, consistent texture that remains pervious to water when compacted.

▮ **Uses:** Bedding material for pavers and flagstones, joint filler for pavers

▮ **Sold by:** Cubic yard

SCREENINGS/DECOMPOSED GRANITE

Byproduct of rock crushing operations. Includes particle sizes $\frac{3}{8}$ inch and smaller that filter through gravel sorting screens. Becomes impervious to water when compacted.

▮ **Uses:** Fine-textured, hard-packed surface material for pathways or patios

▮ **Sold by:** Cubic yard

SLAB STONE

Large section of natural stone that is broad. Many different stone types come in slab form. Stone slabs may be used in their natural form or shaped.

▮ **Uses:** Paving, steps, walls, hearth stones, tables, benches, countertops, and much more

▮ **Sold by:** Ton or piece

SLATE CHIPS

Screened gravel made from fine-grained layered rock, normally dark gray. Particles have a flattened appearance with somewhat angular edges and exposed layering. Typical size categories include ¾-inch, 1½-inch, and 3-inch slate chips.

▌**Uses:** Pathway surface, rock gardens, edging, water features, mulch

▌**Sold by:** Cubic yard

SPECIMEN BOULDER

Irregular fieldstone boulder, often with unique shape, color, or texture characteristics. Sizes range upward from 12 inches to as large as can be moved into place. Sometimes home or garden construction reveals an attractive specimen that can be left in place and worked into the landscape design.

▌**Uses:** Set singly or in groupings, serves as a landscape accent or focal point

▌**Sold by:** Ton or piece

WALL STONE

Any quarried or field stone that is structurally suitable for stacking. Wall stone is sorted according to size categories like Thick Stack Stone, Thin Stack Stone, and Building Veneer. Other names and designations are used to indicate the source, coloration, finish, and other physical or aesthetic attributes that distinguish one type of stone from another.

▌**Uses:** Walls, columns, veneer

▌**Sold by:** Ton or pallet

3

STONE AS A BUILDING MATERIAL

FOUND STONE

IF YOU DON'T HAVE A SUPPLY of stone on your property, you can collect or salvage stone as an alternative to buying it from a retail yard or quarry. "Rocks" that you once barely noticed or may have considered a nuisance suddenly become valuable. Be sure to obtain the owner's written permission when removing stone from someone's property.

STONE SOURCES

▌ Old stone walls and foundations
▌ Abandoned quarries and mill sites
▌ Scrap piles at operating quarries
▌ Areas that have been logged
▌ Building contractors and earthmoving equipment operators
▌ Town and state road crews
▌ Developers and development sites*
▌ Demolition sites and wrecking companies*
▌ Blasting sites and contractors*
▌ Abandoned buildings
▌ Online classified ads (like Freecycle and Craigslist)
▌ Social media groups

*Expect time constraints when you are removing stone from development and demolition sites.

Guidelines for Delivery

Think about where to place the materials before they arrive. You'll need to get to them easily, but you want to avoid obstructing access to the rest of the site. If you can efficiently store and access all the materials for your project simultaneously, ask whether delivery costs will be less if you take delivery of all of them at the same time.

To guarantee that the materials will be placed where you want them, be there when the delivery truck arrives. If the delivery truck dumps your loose stone, some stones will break. Many more will get marred and, depending on where they're dumped, dirty. If this is unacceptable, unload the stone by hand or with a bucket loader. Use a power washer to dull scuff marks and clean off dirt and stone dust.

▲ **In many parts of the country,** the area around your home will yield a treasure trove of stone.

◄ **Some stone yards** will set large stones, such as the ones used in this water feature, as part of the delivery process.

DELIVERY SERVICES. When you order large stones, ask whether the trucker will set them in place. Although companies charge an additional fee for this service based on the amount of time it will take, it's almost always worth it. One way or another, setting stones that weigh 300-plus pounds requires equipment or much muscle and time. Remember that a stone that measures a mere 2 cubic feet can weigh this much; larger stones are much heavier. If you opt to set stones as part of the delivery, prepare the site and, if possible, decide ahead of time how to orient the stones.

Large specimen stones provide a rugged-looking setting for this spectacular backyard water feature.

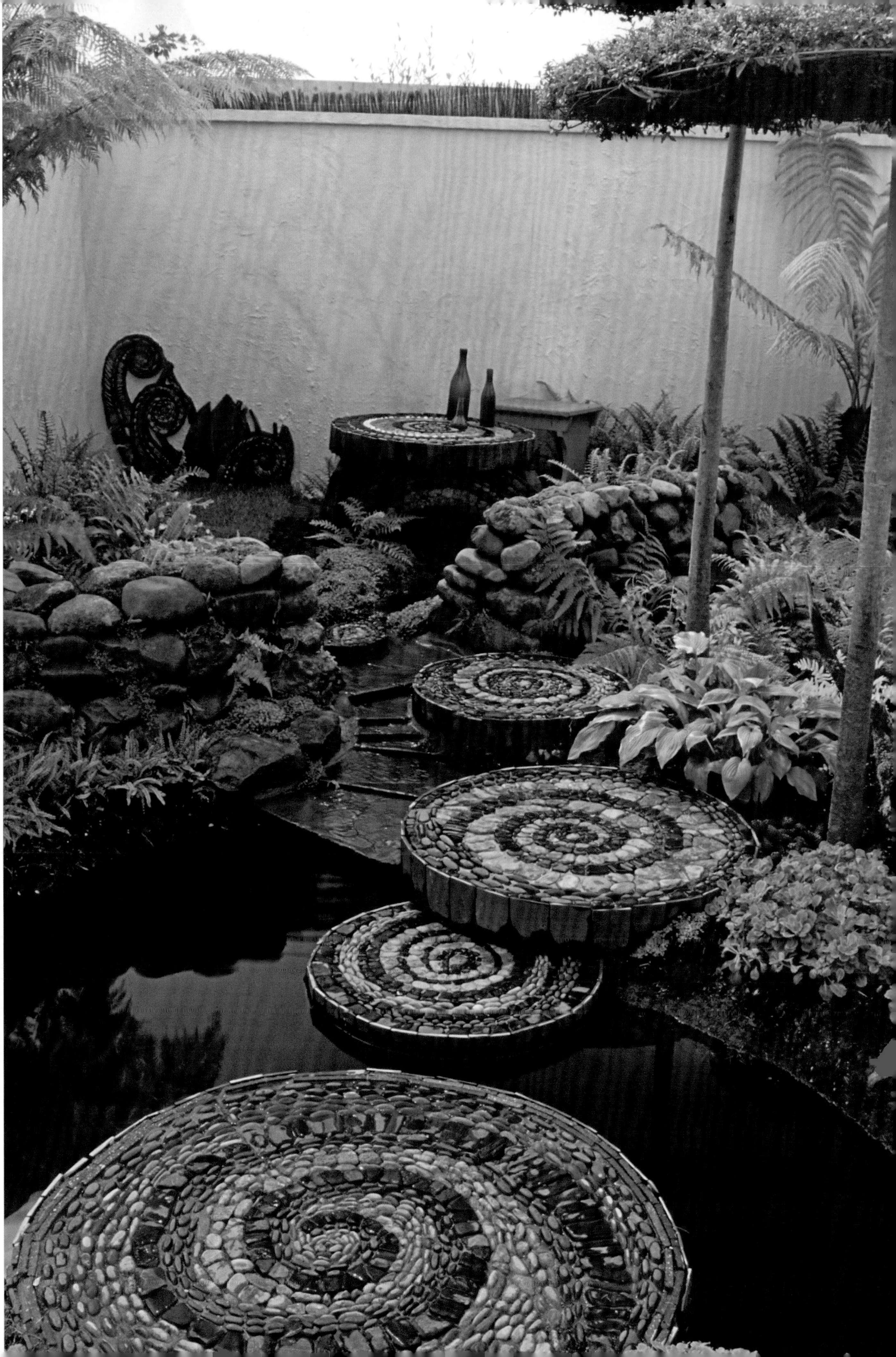

Learn from the Stone

Get to know your stone. Practice on the same type stone you will use in your project. Experiment with how it responds when you split, cut, or chisel it. The better you understand it, the better you'll be able to work it.

For many projects, the quality and overall look of your work depends on the placement of each and every stone. This can be a challenge with any project, but it is particularly difficult when you are building something like a wall. Not only do you have to consider the aesthetic factors, you also have to think about its structural integrity.

Some masons seem to have a natural affinity for placement. But with patience and practice, anyone can cultivate an eye for correctly placing stone. If you take your time with this part of the work, your stonework will turn out to be the pleasing project you originally envisioned. Don't expect to get it right the first time. As with any craft, good stonework takes patience and practice.

CONSTRUCTION TIP

A Real-Life Stone Lesson

A mason I know set a 3-ton (about 3 x 4 x 3 feet) specimen stone at his home. He knew the stone straddled the sewer pipe, but he calculated that the surrounding ground would take the brunt of the load. And for several years it did. But on the morning that he and his family were to depart for a vacation, the sewer pipe collapsed and flooded the basement. After making the repairs, he relocated the stone. He tells the story as a lesson and reminder of the tremendous, constant weight of stone.

◄ **This Asian-inspired garden,** with stepping stones in a striking swirl pattern, offers a private spot for quiet contemplation.

FORMULAS YOU'LL NEED

SQUARE FEET: length x width in feet.

CUBIC FEET: length x width x depth. Use decimals for fractions of a foot: 0.25 for 3 inches, 0.33 for 4 inches, 0.5 for 6 inches. For example, a 4-inch sand bed for a 14 x 20-foot patio would be 14 x 20 x 0.33 = 92.4 cubic feet.

CUBIC YARDS: divide the number of cubic feet by 27. So 92.4 divided by 27 = 3.42 yards, or about 3½ yards.

To calculate the volume of a pile of material, such as a pile of excess soil that you may need to remove from your property, think of the pile as a cone. To calculate volume of the cone: V = pi (3.14) x radius squared (radius is half the diameter) x height, divided by 3.

For example, if the pile is 4 feet high and the diameter at the base is 8 feet, multiply 3.14 x 16 (radius squared is 4 x 4) = 50.24 x 4 (height) = 201, divided by 3 = 67 cubic feet. To get cubic yards, divide cubic feet by 27. Using the example above, 67 divided by 27 = 2.48, or about 2½ cubic yards.

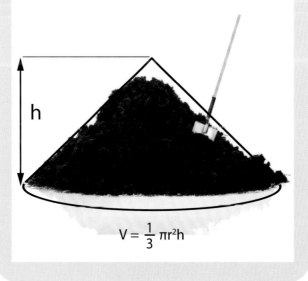

$$V = \frac{1}{3}\pi r^2 h$$

3

STONE AS A BUILDING MATERIAL

4

Working with stone is similar to assembling a three-dimensional jigsaw puzzle. Fortunately, the stone you select and the tools you use to work the stone can help make the task easier. By training your eye to evaluate each stone—its size, building surfaces, and structural qualities—you can decide where the stone fits in your project. By choosing the right tool because of ease of handling and cutting ability, you will not only complete your project but enjoy the rewards of working with stone.

TOOLS AND TECHNIQUES

TOOLS FOR STONEWORK

CONSTRUCTION TOOLS

- Measuring tape
- Marking device, pencil, nail
- 4-ft. level, string level
- Circular saw
- Right-angle grinder
- Framing or claw hammer
- 10-lb. sledgehammer
- Grade stakes
- Mason's line
- Hammer holster
- Tool belt or vest

TOOLS TO WORK STONE

- Mason's hammer – to shape or split stone
- Brick hammer – to shape or split stone (similar to a mason's hammer, but not as versatile)
- Chisels – to split stone and cut flagging
- Points – to chip and direct the force of impact
- Mash hammer – to hit chisels and points
- Rubber mallet – to set flagging and stepping-stones
- Toothed chisel – to refine the shape of softer stones such as limestone or sandstone
- Bush hammer – to smooth or dress irregular surfaces in soft stone
- Masonry blades – for circular saw and right-angle grinder
- Wet kits – for worm-driven circular saws

LANDSCAPING TOOLS

- Shovels
- Digging spade
- Rakes
- Wheelbarrow
- Tamper

Circular Saw & Masonry Blade

Mason's Hammer

EQUIPMENT TO RENT
- Power tamper
- Masonry saw
- Bobcat or tractor/bucket
- Power washer

STONE-MOVING TOOLS
- Come-along
- Platforms and pipe rollers
- Tripod

SAFETY EQUIPMENT
- Goggles
- Gloves
- Upper forearm support air cast
- Steel-toed shoes
- Ear plugs
- Dust mask
- Kneepads

2-lb. Hammer & Chisel

Power Tamper

4 TOOLS AND TECHNIQUES

Tools

The specific tools you will use depend on both the project itself and the type of stone you are using. Besides general construction and landscaping tools, you'll use tools to shape, split, and cut stone. Other tools will help you move and set large stones. For mortared projects, you will also need tools for mixing and applying mortar.

Cutting and shaping tools, such as mason's hammers, chisels and points, circular saw blades, and right-angle grinder blades take the most abuse. Both disposable masonry blades and diamond blades are commonly available for circular saws. The type of blade you choose depends in part on the amount of cutting you have to do. If the work involves a lot of shaping and splitting, you'll need a couple of chisels and points. Sharpen them regularly on a grinding stone, or invest in a 1½-inch carbide chisel that does not require sharpening.

SMART TIP

Tool Sources
If you do not own all of the necessary tools, consider renting or borrowing. Visit LocalTools.org for a list of free local tool-lending libraries, or check out the mobile app store for person-to-person tool rental options.

When planning, remember that stonework can crush tree and shrub roots that are near the surface.

CONSTRUCTION TIP

Leveling Tools

If you can borrow a transit, do it, especially if your project requires extensive grading.

Line levels are inexpensive, but they provide inaccurate readings if not used correctly. The longer the distance you are leveling, the less accurate they are. If you use one:

- Use mason's line for your string
- Pull the line as taut as possible
- Place the level in the exact center of the span
- Reverse the level and split any difference between the two measurements for the most accurate reading

To check the accuracy of any level, use it to take a reading; reverse the level, and take the reading again. If both readings are the same, the level is accurate.

Even if you purchase dressed stone, like the stone in this picture, you may still need to do some cutting to complete your project.

TOOL PREFERENCES

People develop personal preferences for stone-shaping tools based on comfort and control. For example, you might find a chisel and hammer more comfortable to use than an all-purpose 2-pound mason's hammer. Some hammers have impact-absorbing handles, which make them more comfortable to use. A dead-blow hammer delivers more impact than a conventional sledge of the same size. Homeowner-grade circular saws and right-angle grinders equipped with diamond blades can save time, but these tools won't last if you cut a lot of stone or make long cuts. If you have a lot of cutting and shaping to do, you can use a chisel and hammer or rent industrial cutting tools. Specific techniques and tools to shape, split, and cut stone are discussed in the projects beginning in the next chapter.

PREVENTIVE TOOL MAINTENANCE. Over time, the heads of chisels and points can start to mushroom from repeated hits with a hammer. Grind the edges of the head to reduce the risk of cuts from sharp edges. If a sledge or mason's hammer has a wooden handle, wrap wire around it a few inches near the head, and wrap the wire with a strip of tire inner-tube as if it were a bandage. It's easy to lose hammers, chisels, and points in a stone pile, so paint these tools bright orange.

Working with Stone

With the exception of placing specimen stones, the following steps apply to working with stone. While the steps may be the same no matter which type of stone you use, the work is most challenging when the stones are irregularly shaped. Without experience, it may be hard to believe that the quality and overall look of your work really comes down to the structural and aesthetic decisions you make to place each and every stone. This is the challenge of stonework.

Some professional masons seem to have a natural affinity for placing stone. It takes patience and practice, but it is certainly possible for the novice to develop an eye for stonework.

BEFORE YOU BEGIN

The stone is your teacher, so it is in your best interest to become familiar with its character. Experiment with how the stone responds when you split, cut, or chisel it. Consider how variations in its color or texture can enhance your project.

SORTING. After your stone is delivered, sort it for specific uses. If you are building a freestanding wall with fieldstone, sort for large bottom course stones, corner stones, bond stones, cap stones, shim stones, and rubble to fill between wythes. Sort the remaining stones into two or three groups by size.

Every stone has a place. As you sort stone, you build a memory of the stones that you will use later. All through the sorting process, you should be looking for stones with specific structural traits, such as uniform thickness or right-angle faces. You will find yourself selecting others for aesthetic properties that can establish the look or rhythm of your project.

Adjacent landscape plantings, such as this perennial border, soften the hard edges of stonework and help to create a unified landscape appearance.

CONSTRUCTION TIP

Supporting Stones

You must support stones while you are shaping them. You can hold small stones against your leg or in your lap. When you are working on a larger stone or one that needs a lot of shaping, a sand pile or bag of sand is handy. The sand conforms to the stone's shape and supports the stone at whatever angle you place it.

CHOOSING STONE DURING CONSTRUCTION. During construction, evaluate each stone again, but this time to determine the best surfaces for a base, top, face, and sides. Assess the degree of flatness and right angles to the face. Then evaluate how this stone fits to the ones adjacent to it.

For example, in wall construction, you have to consider four building surfaces: the two lateral faces and the top and bottom ones. Besides the stone's surfaces, you'll also need to consider how the load is distributed as well as whether the fit of the stone helps to create a flat bed for the next course. (See "Understanding Gravity," below.)

Another way to select a stone is to evaluate the shape of the space and look for that shape in the stone pile. With practice, you can intentionally create spaces that use the stones you have. (See "Stone Selection," opposite.)

Pay as much attention to the origin of your stones as to the technical considerations when you are placing them. For example, if you have a stone that was partially buried, it will have a distinct color change at the soil line. If you turned this stone 90 degrees, you'd diminish its natural look and aesthetic appeal, even if the shape works beautifully.

ESTABLISHING A RHYTHM. Designers use the term rhythm to refer to the way stones of varying sizes and types

Consider using plants as borders for your stonework, or grow plants in soil pockets in walls.

create a pattern that, though not necessarily geometric, is intentional. Often subtle, rhythm is crucial to the unity and aesthetic appeal of your project. Use rhythm as one criterion to select stones: place them purposefully. Even a skilled mason who is experimenting with a particular effect sometimes dismantles and rebuilds a section of stonework looking for a sustaining rhythm.

SHAPING SKILLS

Deciding whether to hunt for a stone that is a good fit or shape one that nearly fits is often more a matter of work style and aesthetics than of necessity or expediency. For example, in walls and patios, how much the stone is shaped will determine, at least in part, joint size and naturalness—both significant aesthetic elements.

Before you begin to shape a stone, evaluate it again—this time for hardness, grain, presence of fractures, and composition. All of these factors can affect a stone's structural integrity and how a stone will break. Shaping stone is similar to splitting firewood or using a hand plane. Grain and imperfections dictate angle, force, and the quantity you remove.

WORK WITH THE STONE. Work with the grain and fractures, chipping off a little at a time. To locate fine fractures, wet the stone and allow it to dry. A fracture will remain wet longer than the rest of the stone. As you become familiar with how a type of stone reacts to the impact of hammer and chisel, you can adjust both the amount removed and the power of your swing. Listen for auditory clues as you work, too. Sometimes you can salvage a stone if you notice soon enough that it is not breaking where you want it to break.

STONE ORIENTATION

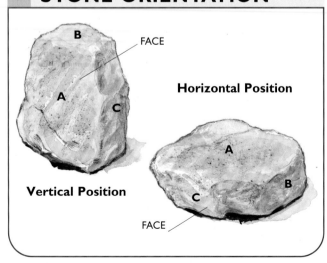

B

FACE

A

C

Horizontal Position

A

B

Vertical Position

C

FACE

STONE SELECTION

4 Options for Completing a Wall Section

CUTTING TOOLS. You can cut dressed and semidressed flagging, step, and wall stone with a chisel and hammer, circular saws, or pneumatic cutting tools. Or you can split them as they've been split for thousands of years—with feather wedges. Each method changes the appearance of the stone's face, giving you good reason to choose one method over another.

Sometimes you need to break up large stones to make rubble fill or shims, especially in freestanding wall construction. To break up a large stone without regard for the shapes of the pieces, hit it hard with the largest sledgehammer you can comfortably swing, and wear safety goggles while you do it.

SMART TIP

Order of Work
Begin your project in the least visible place. By the time you get to the portion that is most noticeable, your technique will have improved.

EXPERIENCE COUNTS. Learning how to see the potential and limitations of a stone is challenging. Strong visualizing abilities can help you gain a working knowledge of stone more easily. But with time and practice, anyone, at any skill level, can cultivate an eye for choosing and placing a suitable stone. Patience, studied observation, and an appreciation for the effort that goes into good stonework make the work more enjoyable.

DRESSED STONE
Many quarries will dress stone so that you don't need to do much trimming to build with it. This stone costs more and creates a less natural look than found, blasted, or rough quarried stone. But the time it takes to fit the stone and complete your project is considerably shortened.

◄ **Make a plan** to keep cutting to a minimum. This patio and walkway uses natural edges, so very little stonecutting was needed.

◄ **Practice using tools** with which you are unfamiliar before beginning your project. For example, assorted replaceable chisel and bit types allow the worker to achieve the desired effect.

► **Modern stone cutters** often use pneumatic tools to cut and shape large stones. A pneumatic chipper is a specialty tool for trimming and shaping stone.

Consult with a landscape designer or arborist about the effects your project will have on the environment around you.

SAFETY TIPS FOR WORKING WITH STONE

- Wear steel-toed shoes, especially if you're working with large pieces of stone.
- Wear a disposable face mask and goggles to cut stone.
- Wear eye protection when chiseling stone or using power tools.
- Rope off large holes or steep grade changes, and mark them with flagging ribbon or brightly colored strips of cloth.
- Wear rubber boots, protective clothing, gloves, and goggles if you work with concrete. Prolonged contact with fresh concrete will irritate your skin.

- Use a tool pouch to carry hand tools, especially chisels.
- Keep your chisels sharp.
- Know the limits of your tools. Don't force them to do what they were not intended to do.
- Practice using tools with which you are unfamiliar before beginning your project.
- Know your physical limits. Use pry bars, skids, winches, and the like to move large stones.

Mortared Stonework

Although mortared stonework can cost up to twice as much as the same work dry laid, safety or aesthetic reasons make it preferable in some applications. Avoid using mortar as a substitute for fitting stone to stone or as an attempt to defy gravity.

For home improvement and landscaping, mortared stonework is more popular in dry, mild climates where the installation costs are lower. But considerations other than cost are also important. Even in climates without frost, the natural movement of the earth can, over time, cause mortar to crack. Mortar exposed to weather deteriorates before the stone. Eventually it will need to be renewed for aesthetic reasons or, in some cases, to keep the stonework intact. Mortared stonework requires supplemental drainage, too. Water can't move through mortared stonework as it does through dry-laid stone.

HOW TO MIX MORTAR

Use a wheelbarrow, mason's mixing box, or piece of plywood to mix your mortar. Combine one part portland cement with three parts mortar sand. Thoroughly mix the dry ingredients using a hoe. Form them into a mound with a well in the middle. Pour clean water into the well, and gradually mix the dry ingredients with the water, working from the center of the mound to the edges. The amount of water will vary with the weather conditions and the amount of moisture in the sand. Measure the amount you use to get a sense of how much you need for each batch.

The mortar should be stiff enough to support the stones but wet enough to spread easily. The following can help you get the right consistency:

▌ If water seeps out of the mortar around the edges, it is too wet.

▌ Test-set a stone on a piece of plywood. If the mortar cannot support the stone with at least a 1-inch bed of mortar, it is too wet.

▌ Palm a lump of mortar in your hand. If it holds together and has a smooth uniform shape, it's wet enough.

◄ **Mortared stonework** is more popular in dry, mild climates where the installation costs are lower and there is less risk of frost cracking them.

▲ **Mortar dries quickly,** so work with no more than the amount you can use within an hour.

▼ **Mortared walls,** walks, and patios tend to be more formal than dry-laid stonework.

MORTARING TRICKS AND TECHNIQUES

▮ Mortar is irritating to the skin. Wear gloves, and wash off mortar immediately if it gets on your skin.

▮ Mortar dries quickly. Work with small batches, no more than the amount you can use within an hour or so. Shade the mortar from direct sun, especially during midday, and cover it with plastic if the weather is hot or windy.

▮ Begin by working with an area large enough for two to four stones. Increase the size of the work area as your skill improves.

▮ Use tarps or cardboard to keep the foundation clean. Use plywood to distribute the load if you need to stand on freshly laid stones.

▮ Slow curing is important. Keep finished work damp by misting it and covering it with plastic for up to seven days.

▮ Clean the surface of stones that get spattered with mortar before the mortar hardens. Use a sponge and clean water.

▮ Mortar stains some types of stone. Check with a supplier, or test your stone for susceptibility to staining.

Mortared stonework is more popular in dry, mild climates where the installation costs are lower and there is less risk of frost cracking them.

Living with Stone

Although stonework installations require little or no maintenance to remain strong and sturdy, some attention will be required to enhance your use and enjoyment.

For safety, hose or sweep walking surfaces to remove vegetative litter and dirt, especially on steeply sloping paths.

Soil pockets in stonework are ideal for planting small ground covers or ornamentals. Unfortunately, blown-in weed seeds can also grow in them. If you can't plant the pockets right away, cover them with plastic and mulch until you are ready to plant. Once the plants mature, it's more difficult for weed seeds to establish themselves.

Mosses tend to thrive in environments with high humidity, moderate to high moisture levels, and some shade. However, some species will tolerate other types of environments. If you want moss to grow on your stonework, search for mosses that are growing in conditions similar to those of your stonework.

MOSS MILKSHAKE. To transplant moss, try this gardener's trick. Crumble a tuft of moss with soil attached in a blender. Add equal parts water and buttermilk, and process until the mixture is the consistency of cream soup (add more water if necessary). Spread the mixture where you want moss to grow. Keep the area moist until the moss is established.

STONE DISPLACEMENT

Even with your best efforts, some of your stones may get displaced. Normal settling or even an accident can cause this.

Dry-laid stonework is more easily rebuilt than mortared projects. Repeated displacement that is not caused by an accident is a sign of an inadequate foundation, too little backfill, or poor drainage.

Allowing moss to grow between pavers, over the period of a couple months, is an attractive and inexpensive way to finish the project.

4

TOOLS AND TECHNIQUES

SMART TIP

Eliminate Moss
Moss isn't always desirable. If you want to discourage moss on your stonework, apply a diluted solution of hydrogen peroxide (½ cup of 3% hydrogen peroxide to 1 gallon of water) to all the stone surfaces until they are wet. Reapply the solution as needed to keep the surface wet for two minutes. If necessary, rinse to remove any residue.

Protect your Plants

Plants almost always suffer if they are close to the area where you are installing a stonework project. Not only does most stonework require some excavation, it also adds tremendous concentrated weight to the underlying soil. Nearby roots are likely to be damaged while you're working.

Ninety percent of a plant's feeder roots are in the top foot of soil—the area most often disturbed by stonework. Although some controversy exists about where a plant's primary feeder roots are located in relation to the trunk, horticulturists agree that compacting or severing a plant's roots can temporarily reduce vitality or trigger a gradual decline.

SMART TIP

Extra Stone

If you are building with an unusual type of stone, stockpile a small quantity of various sizes. It is nice to know that you have replacement stones if an accident ever occurs.

Many stonework projects, such as the dry-laid patio shown here, require few specialized tools, including masonry chisels, masonry hammers, masonry trowels, mortar pans, jointers, and wire brushes.

CREATE A GOOD HOME

DIG THE PLANTS in the late afternoon or on a cloudy day to reduce the stress they'll experience. After digging, to give them a temporary home, you can

- Set them on the ground in a shady spot. Wrap the rootballs in burlap. Cover rootballs with a thick layer of mulch to shield them from sun and wind, and to retain moisture. Use bark mulch, wood shavings, hay, horse manure mixed with bedding, or evergreen boughs for mulch. Water daily or as needed.
- Partially or completely replant your plants in another location. If you partially replant them, cover the exposed portion of the rootball with mulch.
- Pot the plants. You might have difficulty finding a pot large enough for a tree, but many shrubs can fit into a half-barrel or other large container.

Large stones placed in this type of informal arrangement usually do not require any cutting or shaping.

TEMPORARY RELOCATIONS

Create a temporary holding bed for any plants that are in the way or might get damaged during installation. You can safely move many plants, even several species of mature trees. But before you start digging, do some research. Several variables affect a plant's ability to survive transplanting and temporary relocation, including soil type, plant species, time of year, general health, lead time, access, and your capacity to provide care both in a temporary holding area and after the plant is permanently replanted. In the case of large plants, the cost to move them is a significant factor, too. Under the right conditions you can move an 80-foot-tall tree, but it will cost thousands of dollars.

If you need help evaluating whether a plant will survive, consult with a landscaper, arborist, or grower who is knowledgeable about the species you want to move and has experience moving mature plants.

CODDLE DISPLACED PLANTS. Many species of plants can survive in temporary locations for several years if they have good care. Regardless of your relocation method, keep the plants out of the wind and give them similar or less exposure to sunlight than they had in their former location. They will need more water than normal, especially if they are out of the ground or only partially replanted. Some species, such as those with high moisture requirements or coarse root systems, may benefit from being cut back to minimize transplant shock. Check with a knowledgeable landscaper, arborist, or grower to learn whether this is a good preventive measure for your plants.

4 **TOOLS AND TECHNIQUES**

SMART TIP

Emergency Pruning

If you break any branches, immediately prune them back to a joint or flush with the branch collar.

SAVING SOD

To save sod for future replanting, use a square-edged digging spade to cut it into manageable pieces. Although you can roll up larger pieces if soil adheres to the roots, 18-inch squares are manageable for most people. Undercut the sod with 1½ inches of soil. To save the sod, place it on bare ground that has been at least lightly cultivated, fertilize it lightly, and water thoroughly. Water daily, except on rainy days, for two to three weeks.

WORKING AROUND MATURE TREES AND SHRUBS

Large earthmoving equipment compacts the soil and breaks roots. This alone can kill some plants. To distribute the load from heavy equipment, lay down planks where the equipment will be used. Depending on the disruption to plants on the site, provide preventive or remediation care. Water the plants, divert excess water from the area, and fertilize as needed. Wrap furniture-moving pads around tree trunks to protect the bark from impact.

If your excavation comes within 10 feet of a large plant's drip line, you will sever some roots. To reduce shock and minimize stress, cover the ends of exposed roots with mulch, apply a root stimulant either prior to or after excavation, and provide supplemental water. You may be able to purchase a small amount of root stimulant from a nursery stock grower. Watering plants with a diluted seaweed solution can also help them recover from severed roots.

CHANGING THE GRADE

Adding or removing soil around a plant can affect the plant's vigor. How much change in grade a plant can tolerate depends on the plant's general health and its adaptability. For example, soft maples (Acer rubrum) tolerate dramatic increases in grade, but sugar maples (Acer saccharum) do not. Consult a professional to learn how to improve the chances that a mature plant will survive any changes you make.

◀ **Large projects** such as this may require you to move shrubs and trees to another location.

▼ **Quarried stone** set directly into the lawn forms a curving path across the garden.

ALTERING NATURAL WATERCOURSES

When you divert water away from stonework or install drainage, you're changing the patterns of natural watercourses. Plants in the area have adapted to these watercourses and may suffer from the changes you've made. Monitor plants that are downhill from areas where you have diverted groundwater or rainfall runoff. Provide supplemental water if plants show signs of stress. Signs of stress include slowed growth rate, change in foliage texture or color, earlier onset of dormancy, and increased pest infestation.

A stone installation may reduce the soil's ability to absorb rainwater as well. During intense storms, heavy runoff can lead to soil erosion and flooding problems. Mitigate or prevent these issues by incorporating micro pools, rain gardens, or mini wetland areas into the project design.

These shallow depressions slow the water's velocity, capture particulate runoff, and promote water absorption into the soil. Add an assortment of water-tolerant and water-loving plants to maximize the effect.

SMART TIP

Be a Good Neighbor

Remain aware of the mature plants on properties adjacent to yours. If your project changes the direction or volume of rainwater runoff, it could adversely affect plant health. You'll want to provide the same precautions and care to your neighbor's plants as you do to your own. If necessary, let your neighbors know what you are doing and how they can protect their plants.

5

Although paths and walkways direct foot traffic and provide access into and through the landscape, they can fulfill several other landscaping functions. Walkways can divide up large areas, providing more vantage points for viewing gardens. Within a garden, a well-designed path can draw you toward a particular destination. When you use the same material for paths in different parts of the landscape, the paths provide design unity. Paths and walkways also tie preexisting areas to new design elements.

PATHS AND
WALKWAYS

Path and Walkway Design

Paths and walkways can define or create space. For example, a walkway that goes from the driveway to the house can create a planting area between the walk and the side of the house.

The surface quality and overall dimensions of a path or walkway affect its usefulness, so it's important to think about the primary use of the walk early on in the project. Is it to move quickly and directly from one place to another, or to meander slowly as you would through a garden? Do you need a walkway that can accommodate a stroller, walker, or wheelchair? Do you want to be able to maneuver a garden cart or wheelbarrow along the path? Is it a walk or path you are apt to use barefoot? Asking yourself questions like these will help you figure out what kinds of stone are suitable for your project.

► **Lay out** a stepping-stone path by first taking a test walk through the front yard.

▼ **This meandering,** dry-laid stone path leads to a wooden footbridge and a lovely gazebo.

For an informal look, allow moss and grasses to grow between stones.

5 PATHS AND WALKWAYS

COMPLEMENT GARDEN FEATURES

Walkways can complement features such as fences, gates, patios, plantings, and steps. If you consider all the site features together, it will help you make decisions about the location of a walk or path, its design, and the choice of materials to build it. As a general rule of thumb, design paths or walkways to complement the other landscape features in both scale and formality.

MAINTENANCE. Design the walk to make it a pleasure to use with a minimal amount of maintenance. Slope the path to avoid flooding or ponding water. If the path is adjacent to a sloped planting bed, install edging that will keep soil from washing out onto the path stones.

WALKWAY AND PATH BASICS

Although there is no precise distinction between a path and a walk, in general paths are narrower and less formal than walks. A 2-foot-wide walk is sufficient for one person. You may want to consider a walk width closer to 3 feet if it is the main route for wheeled garden equipment. Make the walk a minimum of 4 feet for two people to walk side by side or to pass in opposite directions, though 5 feet is recommended. Main entrances should also be at least 4 feet wide. For wheelchair or assisted access, make walks 5 feet wide. Paths through gardens and to secondary entrances can be as narrow as 14 inches.

It is not necessary to maintain a uniform width for a path or walkway. Varying the width adds visual interest and is a way to provide space for water features, seating, potted plants, or sculpture.

If you are constructing a walk with a uniform-sized paver, lay out a section of the walk to determine the exact width and amount of materials needed. That way you will minimize cutting of the pavers.

PATHS AND PLANTS. Plan your path and adjacent plantings to minimize maintenance and to keep the path from becoming overgrown by the plants that border it. In other words, either use compact edging plants or make the path larger than you want initially so that when the plants mature, you still have the path width you want.

EDGING OPTIONS

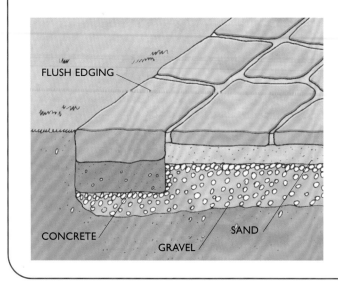

FLUSH EDGING

CONCRETE

GRAVEL

SAND

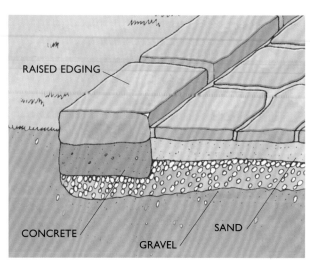

RAISED EDGING

CONCRETE

GRAVEL

SAND

EDGING

Edging can be decorative or functional, and often it is both. For many stone path projects, it is optional.

When edging is used, it is placed along the sides of a walk to define its border and to contain loose walk materials like washed stone or crushed rock. Many landscapers and homeowners use edging to hold stonework and the sand base underneath it in place.

The edges of a walk will get displaced over time if vehicles regularly drive over it. Use substantial edging such as concrete curbs or 6x6 timbers to edge walks that cross or abut a driveway.

EDGING MATERIALS. You can use several types of materials to edge a path or walkway. Wood, collected or quarried stone, pavers, and fabricated concrete products are all suitable for edging. Plastic and steel edging products are also available. The challenge is to choose an edging material that is functional, aesthetically pleasing, and complements the adjacent landscaping.

EDGING COLOR. The color of the edging you select is important to the overall look of the project. Experiment with samples to see how the edging complements other features in the garden. For example, a complementary stone that was used to make a design in a walk surface

◄ **Here is an attractive combination** of a gravel path edged with raised brick, which also create a border for the plantings.

CONSTRUCTION TIP

Wood Edging

Whether you use boards, squared timbers, or peeled logs for edging, choose a species that is rot resistant, such as cedar, redwood, or black locust. Do not use treated wood, recycled railroad ties, or treated telephone poles near food-producing plants.

might also be used to edge the drive, parking area, or beds adjacent to the walk.

EDGING HEIGHT. You can install edging flush with, above, or below the level of the walk stones, or you can bury it. Each method has its advantages. Common considerations for choosing one height over another include aesthetics, what is adjacent to the walk, and the topography in the area of the walk.

Raised edging helps to contain adjacent plantings and keep soil from washing onto the walk. It can also serve as a curb to contain loose gravel or washed stone walks. Flush and recessed edging allows for water to run off easily. Continuous plastic edging is popular because it minimizes the migration of grass from lawn areas adjacent to the walk. Check the manufacturer's specifications for installing plastic edging flush with, above, or below the level of the walk stones.

5

PATHS AND WALKWAYS

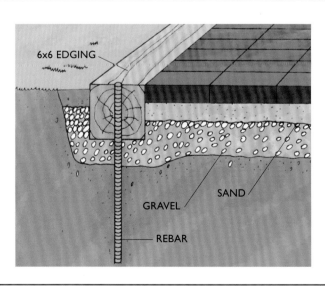

6x6 EDGING
SAND
GRAVEL
REBAR

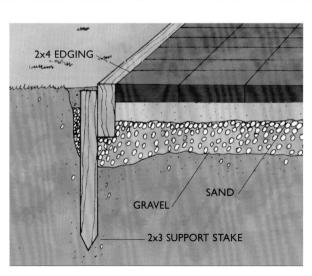

2x4 EDGING
SAND
GRAVEL
2x3 SUPPORT STAKE

SUBSURFACE DRAINAGE

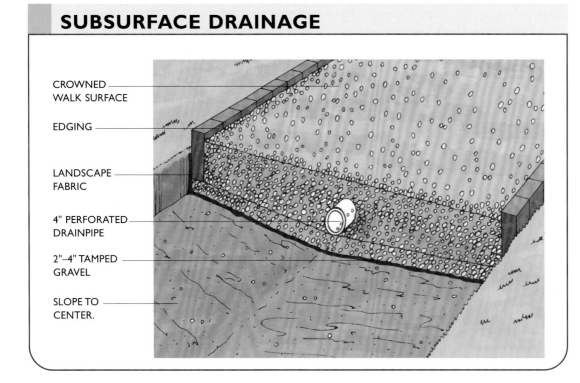

CROWNED WALK SURFACE

EDGING

LANDSCAPE FABRIC

4" PERFORATED DRAINPIPE

2"–4" TAMPED GRAVEL

SLOPE TO CENTER.

▶ **Flagstones** in irregular shapes make a casually inviting entry walkway.

▼ **This footbridge** combines different varieties of stone with wood planking.

WALKWAY SLOPE

Your walk can follow the natural slope of the land if the grade is less than 1 foot of rise in 10 feet of run. If it isn't, then you may want to change the grade, which will make walking on the path more comfortable. You can lengthen the walk (i.e. increase the run) by adding one or more bends. Or, you can add steps as needed to keep the grade at or less than a 1-foot-in-10 ratio. Steps can be added one or more at a time along the length of the walk, or you can construct a flight of steps wherever it makes the most sense to put them. (See "Landscape Steps," pages 126–137.)

Gravel paths and walks need to be fairly level, otherwise hard rains and use will gradually move the gravel from the high spots to the low ones.

DRAINAGE. The layered construction of a walkway or path determines its ability to drain properly. Begin with a base of at least 4 inches of compacted gravel, followed by 2 inches of packed sand, topped with a sloped or crowned surface material. A deeper gravel base improves water infiltration and reduces runoff problems. For chronically wet soil, installing a perforated drain pipe can help. (See "Subsurface Drainage," above.)

You will also want to build up low spots to minimize flooding and puddling. This is a greater concern if your walk material is loose gravel or aggregate.

Try to avoid placing a walk across a slope where it can act like a dam and disrupt drainage patterns. If you must

put a walk across a slope, install 2-inch or larger drainage pipes under the walk every 4 to 6 feet.

If a walk abuts a building, stone wall, or other garden structure, slope the walk away from the structure about ⅛ inch per foot. If the walk is 4 feet wide, the outside edge should be ½ inch lower than the edge against the wall.

CROWNED WALKS. Walkways made of pavers or brick are often crowned, or set so the center of the walkway is higher than the sides. Make the crown (measured from the center of the walkway to the edge) about ⅛ inch per foot. For example, a 4-foot walk is crowned ¼ inch. Flagstone walks are usually sloped across their width about ⅛ inch per foot to shed water.

Stepping-stone Paths

A stepping-stone path is one of the easiest stone landscape projects to construct. Stepping-stones are typically set in lawn, ground cover, bark mulch, or gravel. They are also used in ponds for access to views, to feed fish, or as part of the path network in the landscape. Stepping-stone paths are a good choice in general for informal landscapes, but they can also work as low use or maintenance paths through more formal gardens.

STONE SELECTION

You can use almost any type of stone to make a path. Although stone paths are commonly made with individual stones spaced for comfortable strolling, you can use pavers laid in a pattern instead of a large single stone. Avoid using polished stone because the surface becomes extremely slippery when wet. Using stone dressed to a uniform thickness makes the work go quickly.

LAYING OUT THE WALK

Stepping-stones can be laid singly in a line or deliberately staggered. You can also make a path that is more than one stone wide.

Before you can excavate, you need to calculate how far apart to set the stones. Fifteen inches on center is a good distance that will accommodate a leisurely stride for most people. If you want to test the path for walking comfort, walk the area where you want to put the stones and mark each spot where the center of your foot lands. Use this as

a guide to set your stones. Stepping-stones used in part of a path—for example, to keep you out of a wet spot—can be set further apart, because you will instinctively change your pace when you get to the stones.

EXCAVATE. The depth of the excavation for each stone depends on the thickness of the stone and where you want the top surface of the stone in relation to the surrounding grade. For stones set in lawn, consider placing the stone low enough to mow over. In mulch or ground cover, elevate the stone slightly above grade.

In heavy soils, excavate an additional 2 to 4 inches and backfill with gravel before setting the stones. Save or compost sod by cutting and removing it separately from the soil.

▲ **Filling in mulch** around stepping stones allows the path to blend naturally into the surrounding gardens.

◄ **This edging** maintains the informality of the walk while helping to contain the smaller stones.

► **This stepping-stone path** appears to lead visitors to a magical world.

If your stones are not a uniform thickness, excavate to accommodate the thickest part of the stone. Backfill with sand to support the thinner parts of the stone.

STONES SET IN MULCH. Depending on your overall design goals, you may want to excavate the entire path area, as you would for a walkway, instead of making individual holes. You would excavate the whole area if you wanted to set the stones in gravel, mulch, or a ground cover. Regardless of your method, check the bottom of the excavated areas for level before you start placing stones.

SET THE STONES

After you set a stone in a hole, stand on it and check it for stability by trying to rock it. Stones that are not uniform in thickness are more likely to need fill or sand added to make them stable. Next, use a level or straightedge to see whether the top surface of the stone is at the correct elevation in relation to the surrounding grade. Repeat these steps for each stone.

BACKFILL. For stones set in lawn, partially backfill with the site soil and replant strips of sod, or completely backfill with soil and sown seed to allow the grass to re-establish itself. If you are planting a ground cover, you may want to use a different grade or type of soil for backfill. If you are mulching the area with gravel or mulch, you may not need or want to use any soil for backfilling.

Gravel Paths and Walkways

A gravel walkway, sometimes called a soft walk, is easy and comparatively inexpensive to install. Because a gravel path can conform to any shape, they are a good choice for meandering garden paths. With a gravel walk, you won't have the heaving and displacement problems that you might have with large stones or pavers. Because gravel drains well

GRAVEL-PATH CONSTRUCTION

CROWNED GRAVEL SURFACE MATERIAL

PLASTIC EDGING

LANDSCAPE FABRIC

2" SAND

4" GRAVEL BASE

and dries quickly, it is a good choice for garden paths. An occasional light spray with a garden hose is usually enough to wash away surface dirt.

Gravel walks do have limitations you'll want to consider before deciding to construct one. In heavy traffic areas, gravel gets pushed around and will require raking now and then to level out the surface. When compared with a hard walk surface, pushing a wheelbarrow, maneuvering a wheelchair, or walking with a walker on loose gravel will require more effort, and walking on it barefoot can be painful.

TYPES OF STONE

Stone used for walks is usually classified by texture, either smooth or rough. Rough stones make a more compact walk surface than do smooth stones. Both are available in many colors and sizes. In the gravel path shown opposite bottom, the same smooth shaley stone that lines the lakeshore was used. This is a good example of where the material used also serves a unifying function, in this case tying the landscaped areas to the natural surroundings.

Although commercially available loose aggregate ranges from ¼- to 3-inch stones, the best sizes for paths are between ¾ and 1½ inches. These medium-size stones stay in place better than small pebbles. They compact better, too, and are more comfortable on which to walk than larger stones.

Gravel and crushed stone are typically sold either screened to a uniform size or unscreened. You can also purchase small quantities by the bag at garden centers. For large quantities, you'll want to go to a gravel yard.

SMOOTH STONE. Smooth stone, sometimes called river stone, may or may not be available at a gravel yard. It is usually found at garden centers in a range of sizes and colors.

If you're unsure about the best color and size stone to use, bring home a few samples with which to experiment, and study examples in public parks and gardens.

5

PATHS AND WALKWAYS

For this informal path leading to a back patio, gravel is combined with irregularly shaped flagstones.

INSTALLING WALKWAY EDGING

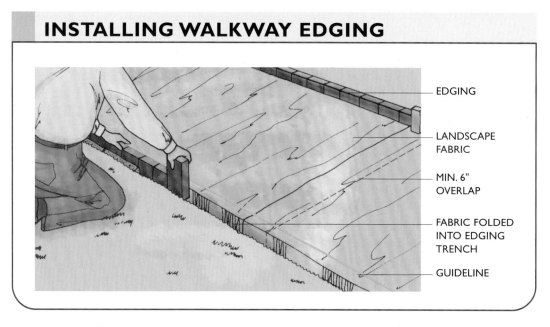

EDGING

LANDSCAPE FABRIC

MIN. 6" OVERLAP

FABRIC FOLDED INTO EDGING TRENCH

GUIDELINE

▼ **Install loose aggregate** in 1-in. layers, tamping between layers to avoid settling later.

▲ **Because gravel tends to migrate,** you may need to add new materials on a periodic basis.

INSTALLING A LOOSE-AGGREGATE WALK

On sites with good drainage, you can place soft walk materials in a shallow excavation without a gravel subbase. Although edging is commonly installed in trenches on each side of the walk, it is not essential. Without edging, however, some of the gravel will eventually migrate to adjacent areas. This isn't much of a concern for low-traffic paths, but you will periodically have to add new material to maintain the look of the walk.

EXCAVATE THE SITE. Begin by laying out the walk

with stakes and string. First, drive two 1x2 stakes at each end of the walk, positioned to indicate the edges of the walk. Then attach string to the stakes to mark the finished height of the edging. Two inches above grade is a common height for edging. Don't level the string; if the ground slopes, the string should slope with it. If the walk leads to a building entrance, make sure your lines are perpendicular to the building.

TRENCHES. Use a flat-bladed shovel to dig narrow trenches for the edging. Dig the trenches deep enough so that the edging just touches the string. Line the trench and the entire walk area with landscape fabric. For curved walkways, install the landscape fabric across the width of the excavation instead of running it down the length. Overlap all seams at least 6 inches. (See "Installing Walkway Edging," opposite.)

EDGING. Before you begin, check your strings to make sure they are at the right height. The strings are your guide to positioning the edging and maintaining a uniform height. Use stakes to support wood edging. For curved edging, use a rope or garden hose to create smooth curves. As you set the edging material, fill behind it with compacted soil. Bed brick or block edging by tapping the inside faces with a rubber mallet.

SPREAD THE LOOSE AGGREGATE

Add the walk gravel in 1-inch layers, spreading and tamping each layer until the material is ¼ to ¾ inch from the top of the edging. The walk surface should be at or above the surrounding grade. You can slightly crown the middle of the walk to improve drainage.

5

PATHS AND WALKWAYS

CONSTRUCTION TIP

Plotting Curves

Lay out curves with two ropes or garden hoses. Outline one side of the curve with a rope or hose. Use sticks cut to the appropriate length to set the width of the walk. Place them at intervals as shown. If your walk is not a uniform width, you can use the same layout technique with different-length sticks to indicate the varying widths of the walk. Outline the other edge of the walk with the second rope or hose. Sprinkle flour or sand or use marking paint to outline the excavation area.

Dry-Laid Flagstone Walks

A dry-laid flagstone walk is set on a gravel and sand base. Properly installed, it will last more than a lifetime with little maintenance. Though the following instructions are for working with flagstone, you can follow the same steps to install brick, Belgian block, or concrete pavers for a walk.

WALK DESIGN

Begin by determining the exact width of the walk. If you are using rectangular pieces of stone in one or more sizes, do a trial layout of several courses on a hard, flat surface, like a driveway. Include the spaces for joints in your layout.

Ideally, you want a walk that is the correct width without creating the need to cut stones. If you are working with irregularly shaped pieces of flagstone, you can skip this step because some cutting will be necessary. However, the more you plan, the less cutting and shaping you will need to do.

◀ **The uses you envision** for your path will help determine its style and the type of stone you select.

▶ **To avoid ponding water,** slope the path to allow for water runoff or install a drainage system.

DRY-LAID FLAGSTONE PATH CONSTRUCTION

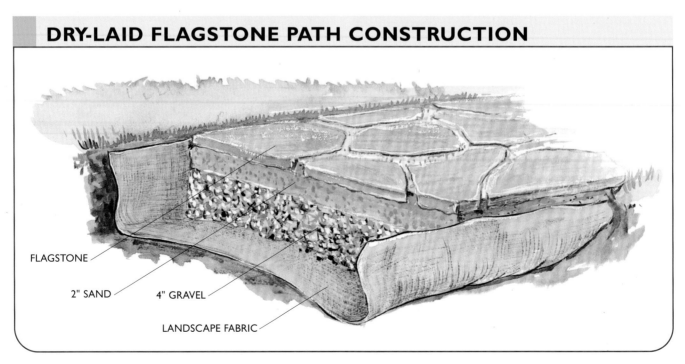

FLAGSTONE

2" SAND   4" GRAVEL

LANDSCAPE FABRIC

LAY OUT THE WALK. Establish the outline of the walk as described in "Excavate the Site," page 99. To shed water, the walk should slope side to side about 1/8 inch per foot. Mark one stake at each end of the low side of the walk to establish the walk's height. Typically, this is about 1 inch above ground level. Use a level to transfer this mark to the other two stakes. From this mark, measure up the appropriate distance to establish the correct slope. Then set your strings to indicate the finished height of the walk.

MARK THE GROUND. Mark the location of the walk edges on the ground by sprinkling flour or sand over the strings or using surveyor's marking paint. Make sure your string location marks are clear, and remove the strings to excavate the area. You will reattach the strings later.

EXCAVATE THE SITE. Use a pickax and shovel to excavate an area about 1 foot wider than the finished walk size. This will give you room for forms and edging material (optional). The excavation needs to be deep enough for 4 inches of gravel (more in a wet site), 2 inches of sand, and the thickness of the paving material. If your soil is gravelly and drains well, you may be able to omit some or all of the gravel.

Once the edges of the walk are excavated to the approximate depth, reinstall the strings so that you can use them to check for the correct depth. Once the area is excavated, use a tamper to compact the subsoil. Install landscape fabric in the bottom and up the sides of the excavation.

LAY STONE IN SAND

Spread about 2 inches of gravel in the excavation; tamp it; level it with a rake; and tamp it again. Continue to add gravel until the top of the form board set on the gravel is level with the strings.

SET FORMS. Drive 2x3 stakes at the ends of the excavation and every 2 to 3 feet along it. Position the stakes to allow for a 2-by form board with the inside face in line with the string that marks the edge of the walk. The forms hold the edging in place and serve as a guide for a screed. Attach the form boards to the stakes with screws.

If the sides of your walk abut a planting bed and the overall landscaping design is informal, you can eyeball the edges or intentionally make them irregular. In this case, the forms are there to screed the sand.

SPREAD THE SAND. Shovel builder's sand evenly over the compacted gravel, and spread it with a rake. Thoroughly dampen the sand with a gentle spray. Fill in and dampen any low spots. Repeat the process, building up the sand so that the paving material will be ¼ to ½ inch higher than the intended walk height to allow for settling.

SCREED THE SAND. While the sand is moist, pull a notched 1x6 screed board in a zigzag motion along the form boards to level high spots and fill in low spots in the sand bed. After screeding, dampen the sand again with a fine mist.

SET THE PAVING MATERIAL. Working from one corner against an edging or string, place the stone in the desired pattern and spacing without disturbing the sand bed. Joints in irregular flagging will vary, but try to keep them consistent within a range: ½ to 1 inch works well for most applications. Trim irregular flagstone as needed to fit.

If you are laying a pattern in courses, mark the walk layout on the forms and stretch a string across the marks to maintain the courses. Check for level frequently. Remove any stones that don't conform or aren't stable, adding or removing sand as necessary. Tap each stone into place with a rubber mallet. If you are working with small-dimension stone, lay several square feet and then place a 1x6 straddling several stones and tap it with the mallet. Repeat until all the stones have been set.

Avoid standing or kneeling directly on the sand bed or freshly laid paving. Place a piece of ½-inch plywood over the paving before you stand or kneel on it. Or prepare the sand bed, and lay the stone in small sections.

▲ **Use a notched 2x6 or a 2x4** attached to a longer board as shown to screed the sand level.

▼ **Set the flagstone** by placing each stone in position and tapping with a rubber mallet.

► **A walk** of square and rectangular flagstones complements the traditional style of this home.

▼ **Design the walk** to make it a pleasure to use with a minimal amount of maintenance.

FILL THE JOINTS. To fill the joints with sand, spread a thin layer of mason's sand over several square feet of the paving. Use a stiff broom to sweep the sand into the joints. Sweep in all directions. Add more sand as needed to fill all the joints. Sweep excess sand into a pile and remove. Lightly spray the walk with water to pack the sand down and to wash it off the surface. Allow the surface to dry; then repeat the process until all the joints are completely filled in and compacted.

REMOVE THE FORMS

When the walk is complete, carefully pull up the temporary forms and shovel gravel along the outside of the walk or edging and behind the landscape fabric. After tamping, finish backfilling with a few inches of soil, decorative stone, or mulch.

Over time the joints may need to be refilled. If a stone heaves or settles, remove it. Re-form and water the sand bed; replace the stone; and refill the joints.

Stepping-stones in Water

You can use stepping-stones into or through a shallow pond or stream to make a path layout that works best for your landscape. Steps through water also give you vantage points that you wouldn't have from shore. For formal gardens, use square or rectangular cast-concrete slabs, large quarry tiles, or cut stone for path stones in water. In a less formal setting, you can use irregularly shaped rocks or flagstones. In either case, you will have to decide on an arrangement for the path stones. As a rule, a random or zig-zag pattern is more interesting than stones set in a straight line. Choose stones that are large enough and spaced close enough—12 to 15 inches between stones—for a comfortable walking stride.

SETTING THE STONES. There are several ways to set stepping-stones in water. The variables are: the depth of the water, the size of the stones, and whether or not there is liner material on the bottom of the water feature. In all cases, it is crucial that once the stones are set, they are completely stable. The first step to assuring stability is setting the stones on undisturbed or well-compacted soil.

You can set large stones with flat bottoms directly into the water. If the stone cannot be set securely without rocking, then you may need to make a nest of concrete to cradle the stone.

If you've installed a flexible liner or preformed shell for a water feature, you will have to take additional precautions to set stepping-stones without tearing the liner. For very large stones, you may need to install a concrete footing under the liner material if the soil is not well compacted. You will also want to sandwich a piece of liner material between the stones and the liner to protect the liner.

ADDING PIERS. In deeper water, you will need to build a pier for each stone. Piers are most easily made out of concrete, brick, or cut stone. Generally, they will need a poured concrete footing for support and stability. Make the footing at least 3 inches larger than the pier on all sides.

SAFETY CONSIDERATIONS. Set stepping-stones high enough above the water so that the walk surface stays dry. Wet rocks are often slippery, and if they're constantly wet, algae or moss can grow on them making them even more slippery. For that reason, avoid placing stepping-stones near waterfalls or fountains. Porous rock such as sandstone is more prone to develop moss than nonporous rock such as granite. Check the steps regularly for any slick buildup, and scrub it off with a stiff brush. Walk across the stepping-stones from both directions on a regular basis to check for shifting or movement that makes the stones rock unpredictably. Over time you may occasionally have to reset stones that become unstable.

STEPPING-STONE OPTIONS

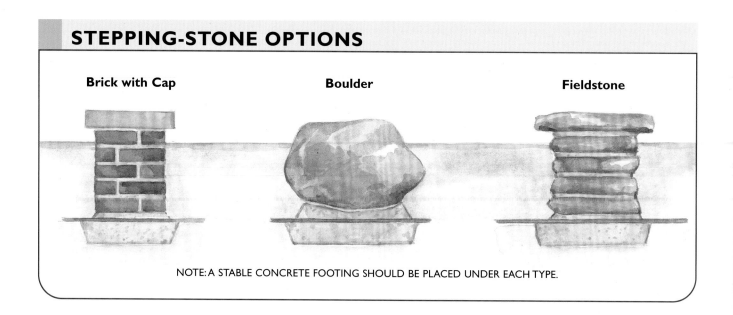

Brick with Cap **Boulder** **Fieldstone**

NOTE: A STABLE CONCRETE FOOTING SHOULD BE PLACED UNDER EACH TYPE.

▶ **Set stepping-stones** above water level to help keep them as dry as possible.

5

PATHS AND WALKWAYS

6

When planning your patio, think about the many ways it can contribute to your outdoor living space and the overall landscape. How can it add unity or help to organize the landscape? How can it improve the feel and use of the outdoor area? Design considerations like these are as important to the success of your project as proper installation. The most common use for a patio is as an outdoor room. A well-designed patio is the ultimate versatile living space—a place where you can play, eat, relax, or entertain.

STONE
PATIOS

Patio Uses

Patios make inviting outdoor living areas, but they can also serve other functions. For example, from a patio you can step up onto a veranda, down to a swimming pool, or you can take stepping-stones that lead to the front of your house. From the opposite side of the patio you might reach stone steps that take you to a lower garden. In other words, its location helps to organize the entire backyard area. Plus, a stone patio provides a protective barrier in areas subject to the threat of wildfire and boosts the home's value.

Building a patio is not difficult as long as you pay attention to the details and complete each step before you begin the next. The patio installation techniques described and illustrated here are versatile; with them you can build durable hard surfaces to use as entryways or courtyards, or even to create a secluded spot away from the house.

Installing a Dry-Laid Patio

Installation techniques for a dry-laid patio are essentially the same no matter which type of stone, pattern, shape, or size you choose. But natural stone that is not dressed to a uniform thickness takes more time to install than uniform pieces because you need to adjust the depth of the sand bed to accommodate the thickest stones. Crazy paving, made of irregularly shaped pieces, and intricate designs also take longer to install than rectangular stones.

As a general rule, a professional spends about half the installation time on preparation and half on setting the stone. The amount of preparation time increases if you excavate by hand, move gravel and sand without a bucket loader, or use a hand-held tamper to compact the gravel.

A dry-laid patio is not attached to the home foundation. The fabric underlayment forms an L shape where the compacted soil meets the foundation, so that it separates the foundation from the gravel layer that comes next.

DRY-LAID PATIO CONSTRUCTION

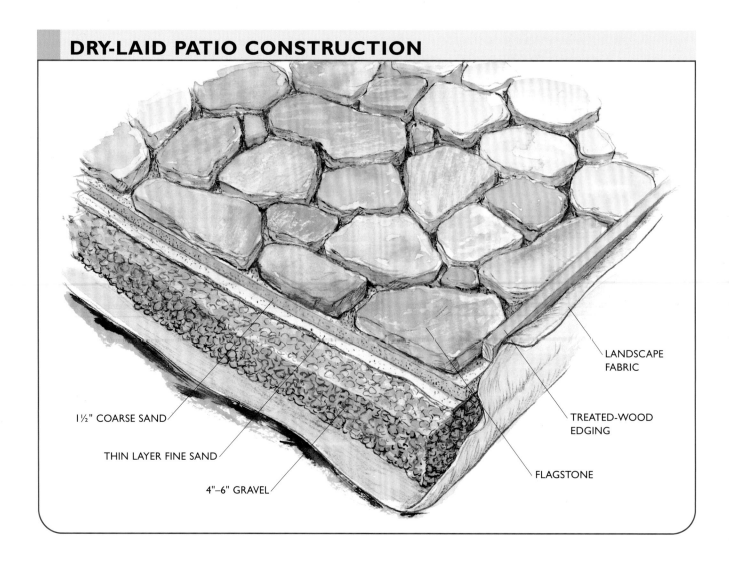

1½" COARSE SAND

THIN LAYER FINE SAND

4"–6" GRAVEL

LANDSCAPE FABRIC

TREATED-WOOD EDGING

FLAGSTONE

TOOL SUGGESTIONS. A masonry saw makes it possible for you to consider building a patio with a complex design, so you might consider renting one. If you do plan a complex design, work it out on paper and make templates for the various shapes. Cut all the stone at once and make a few extra of each shape for spares. During construction, you can use a masonry blade in a circular saw to make cuts. You can also use a chisel and hammer to cut the stone, but this gives the stone a different type of edge.

Irregularly sized joints will give your patio a casual look. Joints of all the same size lend a formal appearance.

6

STONE PATIOS

▲ **Stone provides** a waterproof surface for a patio fountain.

▼ **Stone works well** in most landscapes. Here, flagstone helps tie together this yard's seating and pool areas.

CONSTRUCTION TIP

Grading Basics

To prepare a slope or uneven ground for a patio or walkway, remove the sod and topsoil by hand; for larger areas use a backhoe or bulldozer. Level the subsoil by cutting and adding fill. Bring the grade up to the desired elevation by adding new fill and compacting it to a uniform depth over the entire area. Resist the temptation to add new fill only; this is not a stable base for a patio. For stability you need layers of similar types of soil to minimize shifting, sliding, and heaving over time.

LAYOUT. Begin laying out your patio by marking the corners with stakes. If the shape is irregular, place a rope on the ground to mark the outline. Use layout paint to draw the shape on the ground. (Layout paint is available at building supply stores.) Chalk, lime, and cornstarch also work for outlining but are less permanent and difficult to use if it's windy.

Building a Patio

To mark the perimeter of a rectangular patio, construct batter boards about 1 foot outside the footprint. If one side of the patio is adjacent to a structure, drive two stakes next to the building so that strings attached to them accurately indicate the edges of the patio. Use mason's or carpenter's twine or a substitute that does not stretch. Check rectangular patios for square. Don't assume the adjacent building is square.

If it won't complicate any future construction projects, square the patio to the adjacent wall. If a building is out of square and the patio goes around a corner or is adjacent to an inside corner, you may have to modify the paving pattern.

Mark the corners on the ground. Use a plumb bob, and mark each corner with a painted or flagged spike. To transfer the footprint to the ground, stretch strings between the flagged spikes near the ground. Use these lines as a guide to paint or lime the patio footprint on the ground.

▼ **A single stone design** used throughout this expansive backyard helps to unite the different living areas.

CHECKING FOR SQUARE

HERE'S A METHOD that ensures corners are square: mark one string tied to a batter board 3 feet from the corner; mark the other string 4 feet from the corner; and measure the distance between the marks. If it is 5 feet, the corner is square. It if isn't, adjust the string until the distance is correct.

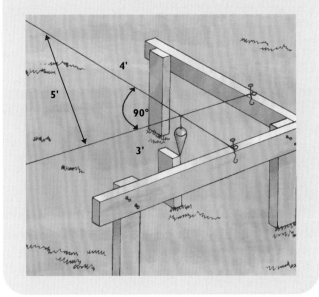

▲ **Get a sense** of the true size of your planned patio by laying out its borders with string.

6

STONE PATIOS

LEVELING

The easiest way to establish level is to set up leveling lines inside the perimeter. It is possible to use the perimeter squaring lines to establish level, but because this can be confusing, it's not a good way to start. Use 1x2 or larger stakes. If the shape of the patio is irregular, set the strings near the edges of the footprint. Level the strings with the most accurate leveling tool you have. (See "Leveling Tools," page 73.) Make a permanent mark on each stake to indicate the location of the line for level. Check the location of the leveling lines before using them: lines inevitably get bumped and tripped over during construction, and animals can also displace them.

▲ **Adjust strings** attached to stakes to provide ⅛ in. of slope per foot of patio.

◄ **In this patio,** several different types of stone are used for a unique effect.

▶ **Patios** made of small-dimension stones will usually require a border to keep the material in place.

CALCULATE THE SLOPE

Patios must slope at least ⅛ inch per foot to drain satisfactorily. On a circular or irregularly shaped patio, the slope can be pitched in different directions. Large patios can be pitched in two opposite directions to minimize the change in elevation from one side to the other. In any case, pitch the slope away from structures and travel paths. Consider the patio's size and shape, the elevation of adjacent thresholds, and the location of the drainage channels. Then establish the slope in whichever way makes the most sense.

ESTABLISHING SLOPE. To establish the slope, you will need to adjust the leveling strings. For example, if a patio is 14 feet wide, the slope from one side to the other will be at least 1¾ inches. Depending on the existing grade, you can establish the slope several ways. You can slide the string up 1¾ inches on the side nearest the house, drop the level 1¾ inches on the side farthest from the house, or make up the 1¾ inches by taking a little from one side and adding a bit to the other. For example, you could raise one end 1 inch and lower the other end ¾ of an inch. To help maintain the slope during construction, place additional leveling strings perpendicular to the main leveling lines.

▲ **A mortared patio** with crisp, neat joints lends a formal look to any landscape design.

6

STONE PATIOS

EXCAVATE THE SOIL

The excavation area for the patio includes its footprint and 6 to 12 inches beyond the footprint on all sides, except where the patio abuts a building or an existing paved surface. Remove any plants or sod within this area. Use the sod to patch lawn elsewhere, or compost it. Dig out the topsoil, and reserve it for grading.

USE A STORY POLE. A story pole can help you visualize and estimate excavation and fill needs when you are preparing a level area at a particular elevation. It can also help you see potentially awkward grade changes at the edges of a patio. Having this information early on in a project can help you incorporate grade changes into your landscaping plan.

EXCAVATION DEPTH. Before you can calculate the excavation depth you need to answer two questions: What is the total thickness of the patio, and where do you want the finished surface of the patio in relation to the adjacent grade? For example, 1½ inches of stone, plus a 2-inch sand bed, plus 6 inches of compacted gravel equals a total patio thickness of 9½ inches. If you want the finished surface to be an inch above the adjacent grade, you will need to excavate a depth of 9½ inches minus 1 inch, or 8½ inches.

USING A STORY POLE

BECAUSE MOST PATIOS are near a house entrance, it's important to learn how to make and use a story pole that includes the elevation of the threshold in relation to the top surface of the patio stones.

To make a story pole for sites that require less than 4 feet of new fill, use a 5-foot-long 1x2. Square one end. Beginning at the squared end, make a mark to indicate each layer of fill and stone needed above the leveled subsoil. For example, you could allow 6 inches of gravel for drainage, 2 inches of sand, and 2 inches for the stone paving. This total is the elevation for the edge of the patio nearest the house. Mark the board 1 to 3 inches above the top of the paving mark to indicate the location of the threshold.

To estimate excavation and fill needs, begin by removing the sod and topsoil. Set the story pole at the edge of the area where the planned patio will be nearest the house. Place a level between the point below the threshold where the top surface of the patio will be to the story pole. Stretch a line or use a board if the distance is more than the length of your level. Check to see how the actual reading compares with the mark on the story pole for the finished top surface. If the reading is above the mark on the story pole, raise the grade; if it is below, excavate. Repeat this process wherever there are grade changes within the area for the patio. In addition to the existing grade variables, the far side of the patio should be lower than the edge nearest the house, at a rate of at least ⅛ inch per foot.

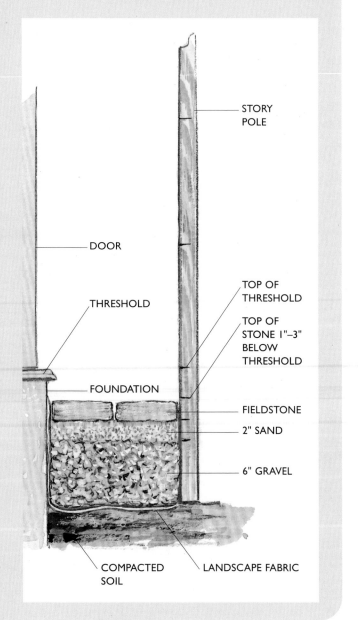

STORY POLE

DOOR

THRESHOLD

TOP OF THRESHOLD

TOP OF STONE 1"–3" BELOW THRESHOLD

FOUNDATION

FIELDSTONE

2" SAND

6" GRAVEL

COMPACTED SOIL

LANDSCAPE FABRIC

When setting stone or pavers in mortar, be sure to remove mortar drips from the face of the stone before it sets.

SMART TIP

Cold Climate Drainage

In heavy soil or unprotected locations that experience temperatures below 0°F, you may need a gravel base that is up to 12 inches thick. Ask a local landscaper to recommend a gravel thickness for severe site conditions.

Use your sloped leveling lines and a story pole to excavate or fill the entire area to a uniform depth with on-site subsoil.

Tamp the fill each time you add 2 inches of material. Consider renting a power tamper for large areas or if you have to add a lot of fill. You can compact up to 4 inches of material at one time with a power tamper.

Lay weed barrier fabric over the graded subsoil, overlapping the joints about 6 inches. The fabric suppresses unwanted vegetation and, more importantly, keeps the subsoil from migrating into the gravel. Soil can clog gravel, restricting its drainage capacity.

ADD A GRAVEL BASE

If you are tamping the gravel by hand, lay it in 2-inch layers. If you are using a power tamper, lay it in 4-inch layers. Use sloped leveling lines to spread the gravel to a uniform depth at the desired slope.

ADD A SAND BED

You can use coarse cement sand or fine mortar sand for the sand bed. Or use a combination as shown in the illustration on page 100. Lay two 1½ to 2-inch diameter pipes on the gravel bed about 4 feet apart. Pull a 2x4 over the pipes to spread the sand to a uniform depth. Maintain the same slope as the gravel.

After leveling one area, reposition the pipes and repeat step one. Fill the spaces that the pipes left with sand, and level to match the grade on either side. Check the entire bed for slope with the leveling lines or a level. Add sand to bring the grade up to the desired elevation. After the sand is in place, re-establish the perimeter of the patio on the sand with layout paint or string.

Use bricks or stones as patio borders or to create frames for sand or gravel.

◄ **Embed pipes** in the sand. Pull a 2x4 across the pipes to level the sand bed.

▼ **A design** such as the one shown here adds architectural interest and becomes a focal point in the overall landscape.

SMART TIP

Make Tamping Easy

When using a hand-held tamper, let the tool do the work to get the most uniform compaction. Don't force or twist the tamper in an attempt to further compact the gravel.

6

STONE PATIOS

DESIGN TIP

Plan Carefully

If you plan to plant a ground cover between the stones of a patio, think about the ratio of stone to vegetation you want. Many ground covers grow out over the stones, hiding parts of them and making the planting area look larger than planned. If you don't want this look, you have several options. You can opt to not plant in all of the spaces between stones; or you can make narrower planting spaces, use larger stones, or choose a ground cover, such as thyme, that is easy to trim.

TO EDGE OR NOT

Edging is optional. It can act as a guide during installation, as a barrier to vegetation, or as a decorative touch. If you install it as a guide, you'll set it below the finished surface and eventually cover it with soil, grass, or washed stone. You can also set it flush to or slightly below or above the finished surface of the patio. There are numerous edging options, but firm earth is the best choice if there is any chance that frost will heave the edging.

► **This flagstone patio** blends well with the home's exterior and the surrounding vegetation.

▼ **Combine patio pavers** of varying sizes, shapes, and colors for an interesting effect.

CHOOSE A PATTERN AND SPACING

A stone pattern can do more than please the eye. It can direct traffic flow, define the edges of the patio, or break up the patio surface to define areas according to their uses. Patterns can also ease a potentially awkward transition.

Experiment with your stone to decide on a pattern and joint size. The joint size for crazy paving often varies from ½ inch to as much as 2 inches, for example. You can lay uniformly shaped pieces as tightly as possible—¹⁄₁₆- to ⅛-inch—or space them farther apart. Use spacers to maintain a consistent width between stones. Spacers are available from tile and masonry suppliers, or you can make wooden ones out of scrap lumber. Make homemade spacers the width of your joints and the depth of the stone, plus at least ½ inch for easy removal.

6

STONE PATIOS

SET THE STONE

Both the shape of the patio and the pattern of the stone-work determine the place to begin laying the stone. The usual location is at a corner or along one edge, but some designs are best started from a center point.

To set a stone, place it on the sand bed and strike it several times with a rubber mallet. Uniform support from the sand bed is critical to keeping the stone from breaking. The larger the pieces, the more important it is to support them completely. If you have any doubt about how a stone is set, lift it and inspect the impression in the sand. Add sand wherever the stone did not touch the sand bed.

Use your leveling lines and a level to check your work as you proceed. If you use stones that vary in thickness, check your work frequently for level.

DESIGN TIP

Formal or Not?

Before you begin laying stone, decide whether or not you want an irregular edge. You can trim the stones along the patio edge to meet the perimeter line or leave them uncut and irregular. An irregular edge is less formal and easier to install, and it makes an attractive transition to a planting bed or border.

Using stone in the manner shown here can be a labor intensive process, but the results are truly unique.

FILL THE JOINTS

After all the stones are laid, fill the spaces between them. Sand and soil are the most commonly used materials to fill joints.

SAND FILL. Use fine mortar sand, which is angular rather than round, to fill the joints. Angular sand compacts well and is disturbed less by foot traffic. Use a broom to push the sand into small joints. To fill larger joints, use a small spade or a bucket. Water gently to compact the sand. Refill the joints as needed to compensate for settling and displacement.

SOIL FILL. Use soil to fill the joints if you want to grow a ground cover between the stones. Choose a weed-free soil mix that contains appropriate nutrients. The ground cover will become established quickly without competition from weed seedlings.

▲ **Tool joints** for a neat appearance once the mortar has had a chance to set up.

◄ **Fill the joints** in a sand-base patio with sand, or allow moss or grass to grow in the joints.

6 STONE PATIOS

Mortared Patios

Many people prefer mortared patios because they have a formal look and provide total weed control. But consider this decision carefully. Mortared patios have some downsides, too. They are more expensive to build because they require a concrete foundation. You will either need to build a slab foundation or have a concrete contractor build one for you. Or you can use an existing concrete surface as a foundation if it is clean, intact, and at least 3 inches thick. Secondly, mortared patios do not flex. Thoroughly evaluate the potential for heaving before deciding to mortar patio stones. Replacing broken stones or repairing sections of a mortared patio heaved up by frost or tree roots can be difficult.

Because they are impervious to water, mortared patios increase storm water runoff. Consider the potential for erosion or flooding problems before building a mortared patio, and include plans for safely managing excess water. A well-placed catch basin or dry creek bed may be adequate.

CHOOSE AND DRY FIT THE STONE

You can use almost any kind of stone to make a mortared patio as long as it doesn't break easily or crumble at the edges. Stone that is fairly uniform in thickness is the easiest to work with and requires less bedding mortar than irregularly shaped pieces.

It is important to keep the foundation clean and to remove dirt and dust from the stone while you are working. The clean surfaces will strengthen the bond between the stone and the mortar. If you use irregularly shaped flagging, test fit all the stones before mixing the mortar. Trim and shape the stones to maintain the desired joint width. If there are joints in the foundation, arrange your stones to avoid placing a patio joint over a joint in the slab.

If you have prearranged your stones on the patio, begin by removing the stones in a 4- to 6-square-foot area. If you are using porous stones that can wick moisture out of the mortar, wet them thoroughly before beginning work.

MORTARED PATIO CONSTRUCTION

MORTAR

FLAGSTONE

1½" MORTAR BED

CONCRETE BONDER

4" CONCRETE SLAB

4" GRAVEL

Your patio should have a slope that allows water to drain away from the house or paved surfaces.

CALCULATING MORTAR REQUIREMENTS

To calculate the amount of bedding mortar you need, multiply the patio dimensions by the thickness of the bed. Divide this number by 12 to get cubic feet. Divide the number of cubic feet by 27 to get cubic yards. For example, a patio 24 feet long x 20 feet wide x 1.5 inches thick equals 720. Divided by 12, it equals 60 cubic feet. Divided by 27, it equals 2.2 cubic yards.

To estimate the amount of mortar you need for the joints, calculate the volume as a percentage of the total patio. For example, a 20-foot x 24-foot patio is 480 square feet. If the joints are 1 inch wide and the stones are 2 feet square, the amount of mortar needed will be $\frac{1}{12}$ of 480 (calculate the mortar on two sides of each stone—in this case 2 inches for 2 feet or $\frac{1}{12}$), or 40 square feet. 40 square feet x 1.5 inches equals 60. Divinding 60 by 12 equals 5 cubic feet, less than $\frac{1}{5}$ of a cubic yard.

Another method to calculate the amount of mortar you need for joints is to fill the joints in an area, say 4 x 4 feet, and see how much you use. Then multiply that amount by the number of 4 x 4-foot areas remaining.

124

▲ **The same type** of brick design covers the patio, walls, and steps.

USE A BONDING AGENT. Before spreading the mortar on the foundation, paint on a bonding agent according to the manufacturer's instructions. Bonding agents improve the bond between the foundation and the bedding mortar. The better the bond, the less likely it is that a section of mortar bed or stone can pop loose from frost or heaving.

LAY THE MORTAR. Mix the mortar as described in "Mortared Stonework," page 79. Begin laying the mortar bed at an edge or a corner. Spread the mortar uniformly to a depth of 1½ inches thick in 4- to 6-square-foot areas at a time. Use the edge of your trowel to make furrows in the mortar.

SET THE STONE. Wipe off any excess water from each stone as you use it. Set a stone on the mortar bed, and tap it several times with a rubber mallet to set it in place. Check for slope and elevation. Add or remove mortar, or use a shim stone to maintain the slope and elevation. The finished mortar bed should be no less than 1 inch thick. As you work, remove any mortar drips and smears from the surface of the stones with a damp cloth. Repeat this process until all the stones are set. Wait 24 hours before grouting the joints.

GROUT THE JOINTS. You can purchase prepared grout in colors or mix your own using one part portland cement to two parts mortar sand. Mix and add water as you did for the bedding mortar. Use a margin trowel, another small trowel, or a mortar bag to fill the joints. Compress the mortar, and fill the joints again so that they are flush with the top of the adjacent stones.

TOOL THE JOINTS. When the mortar holds the imprint of your thumb, you can tool the joints. Compact and shape them with a trowel, an appropriately sized piece of pipe, or a jointing tool.

CLEAN UP. Rub excess grout from the stones with a dry cloth 5 or 6 hours after grouting. Following that, wipe the stone clean with a damp cloth, wiping from the center of the stones toward the joints. Do not wipe over the joints.

CURING. The long-term strength of mortar is dependent on slow curing. Keep the surface of the patio wet for 3 to 5 days. If you can, sprinkle it with water, and cover it with a sheet of plastic during this time.

◄ **This charming** patio effectively uses stone, brick, and plantings to create an urban oasis.

► **A seating area** off of the main patio allows the owners to take advantage of the stunning views.

7

Stone steps come in all sizes. Depending on your choice of materials and the building site, they can be simple or time consuming to build. Stairs made with individual stepping stones are the simplest to build and are adaptable to a range of garden styles. More challenging are such projects as setting large 5-inch-thick granite treads or mortaring flagstone to a concrete staircase—projects appropriate for formal gardens and entrances. Choose the type of project that best suits your needs.

LANDSCAPE STEPS

Step Design

Some people add steps to their landscape because they simply like the way they look, not out of necessity. If your slope is less than 10 percent, that is, it rises less than 1 foot in 10 feet of run, then steps are optional. However, one or more single steps can add texture and interest along a gently sloping path.

All types of steps have a few design considerations in common.

RISE AND RUN

The surface on which you stand when you walk on stairs is called the *tread.* The height or distance from the top of one tread to the top of the next is called the *unit rise.* It is the relationship between the depth of the tread (*unit run*) and the height of the unit rise that makes steps more or less comfortable to use. Typically, the taller the unit rise the shallower the tread. As a rule of thumb for exterior steps, the combined length of one tread and two risers should be 25 to 27 inches.

Similarly, a recommended range for the rise between any two steps is 5 to 7 inches. This gives you a tread depth of between 15 and 17 inches. Many landscape designers favor a 15-inch run and 6-inch rise for garden steps.

FINDING THE RISE AND RUN. Before you can make a decision about the unit rise and run, you need to calculate the total rise and run for the stairs. Rise refers to the vertical distance from the bottom of the first step to the top of the top step. Run refers to the horizontal distance from the front of the lowest step to the back of the top step.

To calculate these distances, drive a short stake at the point at which you want the top of the steps to start, and use a tall stake to indicate the front edge of the bottom step. Attach a string at ground level to the bottom of the short stake; stretch it taut; and tie it to the tall stake. Use a line level to level the string. Measure the distance from the string to the ground at the tall stake: this distance equals the total rise—the combined height of each step. To find the run, measure the distance between the stakes. (See "Step Layout," below.)

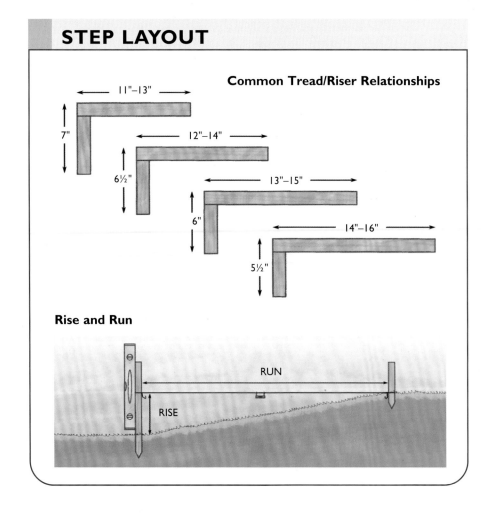

STEP LAYOUT

Common Tread/Riser Relationships

11"–13"
7"

12"–14"
6½"

13"–15"
6"

14"–16"
5½"

Rise and Run

RUN

RISE

▲ **Inspect steps each spring** for damage that may have occurred over the winter. Look for loose stones.

◄ **Ground covers** allowed to spread across the treads add an interesting design touch.

CALCULATE UNIT RISE AND RUN

Once you know the total rise and run, you can figure out the unit rise and run. To determine the unit rise, divide the total rise by the potential number of steps. If your answer is lesser or greater than 5 to 7 inches, you may want to adjust the number of steps. For example, if the total rise is 38 inches and you have five steps in mind, you'd have a riser height of 7.6 inches. But six steps will give you a unit rise of 6.3 inches (38 ÷ 6 = 6.3), well within the ideal range for outdoor steps.

Place large individual stones on a firm base; add well-draining gravel if necessary.

Steps and patios made from the same type of stone create a unified design.

TREAD DEPTH. Now use your unit rise dimension to calculate the tread depth, or unit run. Using the measurements 1 tread + 2 risers = 25 to 27 inches as a guide, in our example, twice the unit rise is 12.6. If you subtract that from 25 and 27 you end up with treads somewhere between 12.4 and 14.4 inches deep.

Now multiply the depth of the treads by the number of steps. Does it equal the total run? Most likely it will not. When your initial rise and run combination doesn't fit into the ideal range, make adjustments to design steps that are safe and comfortable to use. As a safety precaution, maintain the same riser height for all the steps in a flight. For tips on making adjustments, see "Altering the Run," opposite.

STEP WIDTH

In addition to aesthetic considerations, think about how you will use the steps. If they are in a garden where you often walk along with another person, you may want steps at least 5 feet wide. Four feet is a generous width for one person. In a less formal garden, stone steps as narrow as 16 inches may be adequate. The layout and construction is basically the same regardless of the size of the stones you use.

The way the steps fit in with the scale of the surroundings is another important consideration in choosing a step width. For example, steps from a large patio would be wider than steps adjacent to a smaller patio. Steps leading away from high traffic areas are generally smaller than those used as a main entrance.

"Steps through a Wall," below, shows how to make wide steps without having to handle massive individual stones. Many people prefer steps constructed from large stones because of their dramatic design qualities. If you have your heart set on steps made from individual large stones, you will need equipment and an operator to move them into place. If you want to set the stones yourself, you may be able to rent a small bobcat locally. You can also set moderately large stones with a 40-horsepower or larger tractor and bucket.

◄ **This stacked-stone staircase** perfectly balances rough-hewn materials with a more formal design.

► **Narrow garden steps** complement this informal English cottage garden.

STEPS THROUGH A WALL

LAYING UP STEPS as you would short sections of retainer wall is one way to build wide steps without having to use large stones and excavation equipment. This style of step is commonly used to make steps through a wall. The top tread can be made out of one or more stones. Using dressed stone for the tread gives a more formal appearance, but the uniform surface is a desirable feature, especially in high-traffic areas.

Building Steps

After you decide on the size and number of steps, cut and fill the area where the steps will go. The process is similar to cutting and filling for terraced walls. As with most stone projects, the quality of the soil where the stone rests is just as important as the stone itself. Undisturbed, well-drained soils are best for building steps. In all other soils, excavate an additional 4 to 12 inches and backfill with gravel that packs and drains.

THE FIRST STEP. There are three basic ways to set step stones: overlapped, butted, and spaced. Begin at the bottom of the flight, using one of the following ways. The secret to landscaping stone steps is to make sure that the first step is set securely. A good first step provides a firm foundation for the second step and so forth. Follow these guidelines.

▮ The front edge of the first tread may rest on the hard surface of a patio or walkway.

▮ Excavate and set a base stone that is level with or slightly above the adjacent grade.

▮ Remove the topsoil; replace it with gravel, sand, or stone; and set your first step on it. Add 4 to 6 inches of gravel—more if you are building on slow-draining soil.

▮ Create a landing area with a different rise than the rise between steps.

TYPES OF STEPS

Spaced

Overlapping

Butted

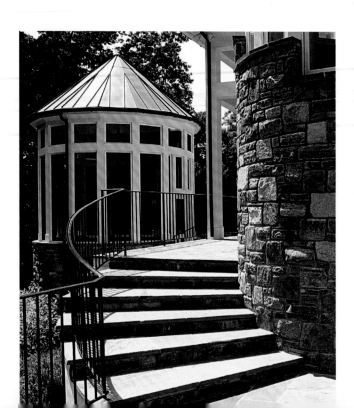

▲ **Stairs made of dressed stone** add texture and color to this front entrance.

◀ **Mortared steps** require a concrete base. Include the thickness of the mortar bed in rise/run calculations.

Each of these steps is actually a large landing, which is acceptable for landscape steps.

BUILT-UP STEP CONSTRUCTION

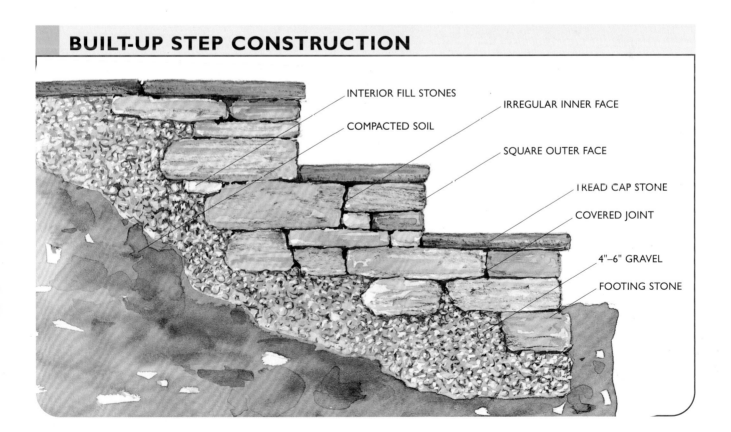

INTERIOR FILL STONES

COMPACTED SOIL

IRREGULAR INNER FACE

SQUARE OUTER FACE

TREAD CAP STONE

COVERED JOINT

4"–6" GRAVEL

FOOTING STONE

SET THE REMAINING STEPS. Once the first step is set, continue setting the steps, using a mallet to firmly bed each stone. Check your work to maintain the same rise between the steps.

Inspect the steps after a hard rain, and make adjustments if a step rocks when you step on it. In climates with freezing temperatures, inspect steps each spring for dislodged stones.

SMART TIP

Using Undressed Stone
If you use fieldstone or undressed quarry stone for landscape steps, adjust the depth of your excavation so that the rise between the steps remains constant.

7

LANDSCAPE STEPS

▲ **Adding landings** to your steps makes the climb more comfortable, and they provide a way to adjust the rise-and-tread relationship.

◄ **These steps** may not be necessary, but they add texture and interest to the area.

MORTARED STEPS

Steps made with mortared flagging or pavers require a concrete foundation. However, before you can install the foundation, you must know the thickness of the stone in order to calculate the rise and run of the foundation. Add 1 to 1½ inches for mortar to your calculations.

If you use pavers, adjust your dimensions to use full-size pavers. If you use random-sized flagging, test-fit the stones before mixing the mortar.

8

Combining water and stone in landscape design has been popular for millennia. Even a small amount of water in the landscape can have a large impact on the overall design. While the importance of water features in the landscape varies from person to person, the life-giving property of water is undeniable and affects how the viewer perceives the landscape design as a whole. Although your local climate will influence composition and formality, you can integrate this revered combination into any landscape.

STONE AND WATER FEATURES

Use large stones to secure the liner of a man-made pond or to enhance a natural pond or stream.

Water Features

Small water features are relatively inexpensive and easy to install, yet they can have a big impact on the landscape. You can install water bowls and low-flow, gravity-fed fountains and other features virtually anywhere. Water features that rely on pumps also provide an environment for water-loving plants that would otherwise be impossible to maintain.

Circulating pump kits available at home centers and garden centers make the installation of water features such as streams, ponds, and waterfalls relatively straightforward. Some kits offer the opportunity to combine features, such as a pond with a fountain or a waterfall with a stream.

To create a quick garden accessory, fill an old birdbath with rounded river stones.

Make a Concrete Water Bowl

A stone water bowl is an easy way to add a water feature to your landscape. They can be pretty expensive to purchase, especially large ones. However, you can create a water bowl out of concrete for a fraction of the cost of a stone bowl. It's a simple do-it-yourself project with materials and tools that are readily available at any hardware or home improvement store.

Almost any type of bowl will work for this project. However, bowls with smooth, tapered sides release easier from the cured concrete. In this project, two stainless steel bowls measuring 17 inches and 14 inches in diameter were used.

This concrete water bowl adds to the beauty of this backyard garden.

TOOLS AND MATERIALS

- 2 bowls (one must be approximately 2 inches smaller in diameter)
- Petroleum jelly
- Concrete mix
- Water
- Trowel
- 5-gallon bucket or wheelbarrow (for mixing concrete)
- Scrap wood (spanning the diameter of largest bowl)
- Large rocks or an extra bag of concrete (for weight)
- Heat gun
- 80-grit sandpaper
- Work gloves and eye protection

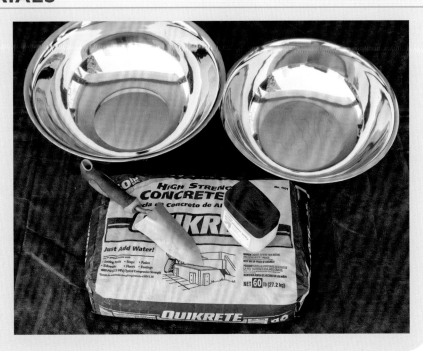

MIXING THE CONCRETE

You will need to mix enough concrete to fill the larger bowl halfway up. You can estimate it, but if you want to be more accurate, an easy way to estimate how much concrete you need is to use the water displacement method.

1. Fill the larger metal bowl with water, and displace the water with a smaller bowl. Pour the remaining water into the bucket. This volume is roughly how much concrete to mix. Mark the water line in the bucket, then dump out the water. Add concrete mix to the mixing bucket to the height of your premeasured line. Add water and mix.

2. You'll know the ratio is correct when the concrete resembles cake batter—not too thick but not too thin. Making the mix thinner will result in a smoother finish but takes longer to cure and is more susceptible to bubbles.

POURING THE BOWL

3. Grease the inside of the larger bowl and the outside of the small bowl with petroleum jelly. Be sure to coat any surface that could possibly come into contact with the concrete, including the underside of the smaller bowl's rim. Other release agents may work better for different surfaces, but petroleum jelly is inexpensive, will not discolor the concrete, and works well with most materials.

Pour the concrete mix into the large bowl. Give it a gentle tap to release the air bubbles. Use the trowel to mold a broad circular impression that will help center the placement of the smaller bowl.

4. Press the small bowl downward into the middle of the concrete mix. Use a firm, steady rocking motion to work it in until the mix reaches the height of the rim.

At this point, the rims of the inner and outer bowls should be nearly level. Scrape off any excess concrete that comes out from between the bowls and smooth the concrete surface.

5. Place a board across the top of the bowls. Place the rocks or another bag of concrete to weigh it down.

FINISHING THE BOWL

Allow the concrete to set up for 24 to 48 hours. The longer you wait, the harder the concrete will be and less susceptible to damage. Do not wait longer than 48 hours to remove the molds.

Once the concrete has hardened, remove weights and board. Use a heat gun or hair dryer to warm the sides and bottom of the bowl. The heat will soften the petroleum jelly and allow the bowl to slide out. Remove the inner bowl first, then turn the bowl upside down to remove the outer bowl.

6. If needed, sand the bowl with 80-grit sandpaper.

MAINTAINING THE WATER BOWL

Because the water in a bowl is stagnant, you will need to change it occasionally. If unwanted moss or lichen grow on the bowl, remove it with a brush. No soap is needed. Use a soft-bristled brush on soft stone.

In climates with below-freezing temperatures, empty water bowls in the fall to reduce the risk of fracturing the stone from freezing water. Tip the bowl upside down; cover it with a tarp; or cover the basin with a piece of plywood to keep out snow and rain.

Constructing a Fountain

Stone fountains come in all sizes, from a dinner-plate-size basin to a prominent garden feature 4 feet or more across. You can install these fountains in a lawn, in a flower bed, or on a terrace or courtyard. Fountains are popular additions to sitting areas, and for centuries they have been installed near house entrances in hot, dry climates.

FOUNTAIN TYPES. Because the reservoir is buried, a recirculating water feature that resembles a bubbling spring is a good choice for households with small children. A boulder or pebble fountain is easy to assemble and is adaptable to any landscape aesthetic. They can contribute both moisture and a cooling effect in the area immediately surrounding the fountain. If you have access to electricity, you can install this type of fountain wherever you can excavate a hole large enough for a 5-gallon pail. You can also create the reservoir from a broader, shallower container with a similar volume or form a basin made of flexible pond liner material.

STONE FOR THE FOUNTAIN

Stone yards often stock large, predrilled boulders for fountains, or they will custom drill to your specifications. There are many variations of the boulder fountain, including boulders with a basin carved out, a stone bowl, or a basin with a hole drilled in it and tooled sculptural pieces of stone. An old millstone or an arrangement of stones can also be used with the hardware for a boulder fountain.

Smooth, worn stones, sometimes called river stone, are typically used for pebble fountains.

◀ **Create a custom garden fountain** by having specimen stones drilled to hold pipes. The pumps are buried in the base.

▶ **Strive for a natural look** when creating a water feature. Note how the top piece pushes the water away from the wall.

PUMP ASSEMBLY

Vertical gusher spouts or bubblers are usually used with fountain-style water features. They can be adjusted from 3 to 24 inches or higher depending on the size pump you use. If you have questions about matching the size of the pump to the fountain, discuss the project with the fountain supplier. As with any fountain, you need to have easy access to an electrical outlet with GFCI protection.

INSTALLING THE PUMP

Begin the installation by digging a hole slightly larger than your reservoir. (See "Fountain Construction" opposite.) A 5-gallon plastic pail works well as a reservoir. Place the reservoir into the hole, and check to make sure it is plumb. Backfill the hole with soil, and contour the soil at grade level to create a basin that will funnel the water back to the reservoir.

Set the fountain assembly in the reservoir, and drill a hole in the side of the pail near the top for the electrical cord. Place a rectangle of flexible liner material (pond liner or heavy plastic sheeting) over the reservoir, pushing the material down slightly into the pail. The liner material should extend far enough beyond the edge of the reservoir to serve as the catch area to return the water to the reservoir. Use scissors or a knife to cut an 8- to 10-inch X-shaped hole in the liner centered over the reservoir.

Place a piece of wire mesh (at least 10 inches larger than the diameter of the reservoir) over the liner. Cut a hole in the mesh large enough for the vertical pipe that connects to the fountain pump. For pebble fountains, trim the pipe if needed so that the stones will hide it. Test the assembly by filling the reservoir with water and following the instructions in the fountain kit to adjust the flow rate of the water.

FOUNTAIN MAINTENANCE

The amount of water your fountain will lose to evaporation will depend on how often you run the fountain and the ambient temperature. Using a stick, check the level of the reservoir frequently until you can establish a refilling schedule.

ALGAE. You can remove algae that builds up on the fountain stones by scrubbing them with a soft-bristled brush.

FREEZING. Empty the reservoir before freezing temperatures can turn the water to ice. Check the reservoir if you have a midwinter thaw or rain. Remove any water that accumulates from groundwater runoff.

◀ **Here's a new slant** on a traditional fire pit. Rather than a flame at the center of the seating area, consider a fountain as the focal point.

▶ **Some fountains** just make pleasing sounds, others are works of art. This unusual sculpture was created from a single slab of stone.

▼ **A bubble fountain** turns a typical pond kit into a dramatic focal point. Ready-made kits are available at garden-supply stores.

FOUNTAIN CONSTRUCTION

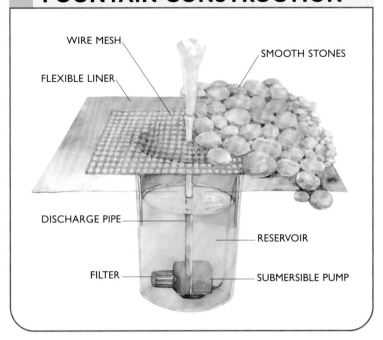

WIRE MESH

SMOOTH STONES

FLEXIBLE LINER

DISCHARGE PIPE

RESERVOIR

FILTER

SUBMERSIBLE PUMP

8

STONE AND WATER FEATURES

Dry Streambeds

A dry streambed is a desirable garden feature that provides visual interest and often serves more than one function. It can create space to display favorite plants, provide a solution to a difficult grade change, disguise a drainage channel for heavy rain events, and of course, create the illusion of water where it is impractical to install a water feature.

DESIGN

A dry streambed mimics nature, so let nature be your guide in designing one. Notice how rocks in or adjacent to a stream are dispersed when the water moves at different speeds, and when the terrain is steep or level. Experiment with stones of different sizes and shapes and their placement. Although some trial and error is inevitable, place your stones and plants with both nature and your design goals in mind to achieve the most naturalistic results.

Flank a planting bed with a flowing river of stones to separate one area from another.

SMART TIP

Bends in the River
Use bends in a streambed to draw the eye to other garden features, such as a specimen plant or a viewing spot with seating.

INSTALLATION

Stone in a dry streambed has three uses: it forms the edge or bank of the stream; it takes the place of water; or it makes the streambed itself. Usually, stone for a dry streambed is used 'as is' and is less expensive than wall or patio stone.

Any changes you make after the initial installation can usually be done with hand tools. In fact, you can install many dry streambeds with a shovel, pry bar, and wheelbarrow. Low-tech installation and relatively inexpensive materials make a dry streambed an ideal project for a homeowner with little do-it-yourself experience.

CONSTRUCTION TIP

Installation Savvy

▮ Use hose or a rope to lay out the shape of the streambed you desire.

▮ Use a plastic barrier under the streambed for weed control.

▮ Set large boulders and rocks first.

▮ Cover any areas that are not planted at the time of construction with plastic and mulch until you are ready to plant. This will reduce erosion and control weeds.

▲ **Vary the width** and the types of stones used to add interest to your dry streambed.

◀ **Dry streambeds** can help lead the eye from one landscape feature to another, unifying the design.

THE NATURAL LOOK

THE FOLLOWING design guidelines will help you construct a natural-looking dry streambed:

▮ Choose a layout that fits the topography and natural drainage patterns of the site.

▮ Change the character of the streambed if it goes through different parts of the garden. For example, use larger angular stones on a steep grade to indicate a falls.

▮ Vary the width of the bed. Add a beach or dry pond for visual interest.

▮ Vary the depth and steepness of the banks for visual interest and to enhance plantings.

▮ Make islands of vegetation or stone.

▮ Place stepping-stones or a bridge across the streambed.

▮ Use shadows from nearby foliage plants to mimic rippling water.

9

Nowhere is the popularity of landscaping with stone more evident than in the increasing use of large stone. You can use large stone to imply or intentionally mimic natural formations, create a mood, convey a message, or construct functional garden features. At the same time, their shapes and mass add dramatic texture, beauty, and character to the landscape. With greater access to earthmoving equipment, cranes, and bobcats, homeowners can now consider landscaping with large stones. As a note, placing larger stones requires heavy machinery and may require professional expertise for best results. If your project requires outside involvement, plan for extra costs.

SETTING LARGE
STONES

Explore the Possibilities

In the project shown opposite, a hole was blasted in ledge for part of the house's foundation. Much of the stone came out of the ground in ½- to 2-ton pieces. The stone's wealth of color, texture, and shape appealed to the homeowners and greatly influenced their landscaping plans.

Their primary landscape goal was to feature, not hide, the fact that the house was built on top of ledge. All the functional elements, such as the entrance walk, drive, retainer walls, and grade changes, were constructed with this goal in mind. Native plants were used extensively to complement and enhance the wooded, rocky site.

CREATING FOCAL POINTS. When planning your project, bear in mind that large stones are focal points within a landscape. In a strong composition, there is also a dynamic relationship between the stones in a grouping. As a designer, you want to figure out how to build those relationships into a visually pleasing whole and tie the composition to the surrounding landscape.

CONSTRUCTION TIP

Burying Stone

When you work with large stones, you often bury one-third or more of each stone. Dig test holes on the site early on in the planning stage, before you buy stone, to make sure your site can accommodate your design. If your soil is shallow, sometimes you can substitute flat-bottomed stones, provided you can make them stable and secure.

Trying to re-create nature is the most challenging kind of project you can attempt with large stone. The more natural you want the stone to look, the more carefully and intentionally you must place it. A thoughtless placement will look like one forever.

STONE AND OTHER FEATURES. When a composition is part of an obvious constructed element, such as a walkway or entrance, it is a focal point much like a piece of sculpture. You want it to fit in terms of scale, color, shape, and surface quality, but your emphasis is on a visually engaging feature, not necessarily a natural one. Which is not to say that you ignore the fact that you are working with a natural material. Successful installations, even obviously constructed ones, contain some natural essence of the stone—how it ages, breaks up, lines a streambed, forms a mountain—something that is authentic and recognizable as true about stone in nature.

Incorporating the size, shape, and surface qualities of your stone is as important as the precise location and angle of each stone. In addition to the design information in Chapter 1, use the following information to test and develop your ideas for a composition using large stone.

◀ **Plan tree and stone combinations** based on the estimated size of the tree at maturity.

▶ **Proper drainage** on an incline helps provide stability for the stones you set.

RULE-BREAKER DESIGN

THE DESIGN at right is a good example of how logic and site-specific traits should prevail over rules of thumb and generalizations. In this case, the recommendation to bury ⅓ of the stone would interfere with the design. Just beyond the cultivated area that includes this composition, natural boulders of a similar size sit on top of the ground, as if someone had pushed them over the steep bank that encloses, and is part of, the garden. There is also a large natural rock area that you either pass or see ahead of you as you approach this stone grouping. From either direction, the grouping ties the pre-existing site features to the cultivated ones. The composition also makes a more subtle contribution, marking the lowest elevation and the turning point at this end of the garden.

Rely on the site to help guide your design choices when placing large stones.

Basic Shapes

The strongest defining characteristic of stone is its shape. Hence, the shapes of the stones you use make a valuable contribution to your composition. If the composition is only viewed from a distance, then you will rely even more on shape to make the composition effective.

Natural stone has varying degrees of rounded or angular edges and can be grouped into one of six basic shapes. The following descriptions of stone shapes refer to the appearance of the stone after it is installed, or its effective shape. When you select stone, you must consider how much of it will be buried and how that will alter its shape.

VERTICAL OR UPRIGHT

Vertical stones appear distinctly taller than they do wide. They are often used to catch or direct the viewer's eye, to help frame the composition, or to add 'backbone,' emphasis, or strength. Using several vertical stones can easily create a border or boundary. A single medium to large vertical stone, particularly one with an unusual surface, is highly sculptural and can evoke serenity and strength.

HORIZONTAL

Three basic stone shapes fit under the general heading of horizontal. For the sake of discussion, they are identified as large, low, and wedge.

Large horizontal stone is unmistakably wider than it is tall and is often dominant in a composition. Large horizontal stone with angular edges is a good choice for a rugged dramatic waterfall, or to create a natural-looking rocky outcrop. Using rounded stone gives a warmer, aged feel to an installation. In the featured project (page 145), several large horizontal stones are used to make a gradual grade change on one side of the house.

Low horizontal stone can be a smaller version of large horizontal stone, or it can be very low flat-topped stone most often used for steps or edging. In a composition, low horizontal stone is less dominant than larger stone, whether it is horizontal or vertical. Nevertheless, one or more can be integral components that contribute depth, balance, detail, and fullness to an installation.

Wedge-shaped stone can be any size and typically has a rounded worn surface that evokes restfulness or tranquility. Its distinguishing characteristic is an obvious slope or incline that is prominently featured in the composition.

BLOCKY OR CHUNKY STONE

Blocky or chunky stone is used in all sizes. It is cube-like in form, though more often slightly taller than wide. This is a versatile shape with which to work and is a strong presence in a composition. You can use it peripherally or as a central component to add depth, cohesion, density, and stability to a composition.

ARCHING

Arching stone is less common and for that reason needs to be used with the utmost care to be integrated into a composition. Arching stone has a distinctive bend that strongly conveys movement, direction, or energy. It is distinctly longer in one direction than the other and can be oriented vertically or horizontally. In a composition, arching stone can easily lead the viewer's eye to a focal point or can direct foot traffic.

This landscape design incorporates chunky, arching, and horizontal stones.

STONE ORIENTATION

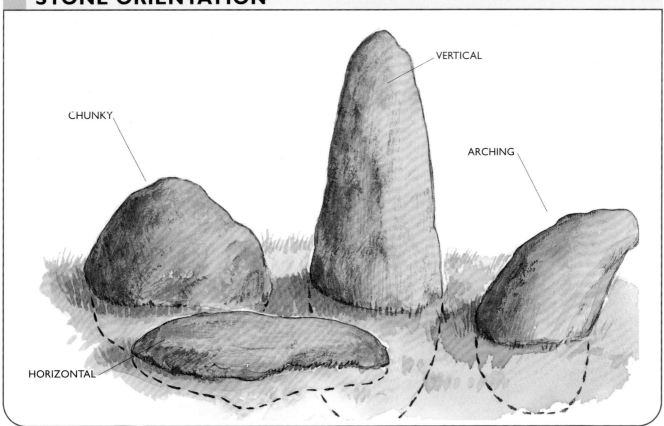

Surface Qualities

The surface quality of stone varies widely. The degree of roundness or angularity of the edges is the most pronounced surface quality. Other common surface qualities are fracture lines or fissures, pitting, and distinctive layers. Since stone is not homogeneous, there may be variations in surface quality when a stone is made up of more than one type of rock. In the Northeast for example, whitish streaks of quartz are commonly found in stone.

In a composition, use surface qualities to engage the viewer and contribute authenticity, unity, or logic. As an example, consider the "lines" that are created by the layers in sedimentary stone. If you set these stones with the "lines" going off in all directions, the composition will have a chaotic quality. Perhaps it would appear whimsical or playful, which is fine if that's the effect you want. However, this arrangement would not work if you were trying to mimic a natural formation, because in nature the striations in a given type of stone go in the same direction. The above example also illustrates that surface quality can contribute to the mood the composition is designed to evoke.

On large projects, draw your ideas in plan form before setting the stone.

USING LARGE STONES

YOU CAN ARRANGE large stones to serve a practical function, resemble or imply a natural form, evoke a mood or movement, or convey a message or information. Below are some examples for each of these uses of large stone.

NATURAL FORMS
Island
Peninsula
Mountains/Hills
Streambed
Waterfall
Trees/Flowers
Fish, Dragons, Birds

FUNCTIONAL—ACTUAL OR IMPLIED
Bridge
Gate
Border
Retaining Wall
Step
Dam

MOOD OR MOVEMENT
Flowing or Swimming
Awakening
Harmony
Humor
Illusion
Strength
Tranquility
Stillness
Permanence
Eternity
Family

MESSAGE OR INFORMATION
Ruins
Guardian or Protector
Ceremony
Beckoning or Welcoming
Sculpture
Boundary
Direction

▲ **This specimen stone** in a Japanese garden conveys welcome to visitors.

▼ **An enormous specimen stone** is the focal point in this Southwest garden design.

9

SETTING LARGE STONES

Creating an Arrangement

Nuances of placement are just as important as understanding how the qualities of the stone itself contribute to your composition. The placement of the stone and the quantity you use also affect the mood or tone of the composition. Will it be grand, sparse, energetic, or tranquil? Once you have a mood or tone in mind, you must somehow integrate it with the degree of naturalness you want the composition to have.

RELY ON EXPERIENCE. While arranging large stone may be a new endeavor, you can draw on your experience in arranging and decorating rooms to guide you through the process. The key considerations include combining large and small components, color, orientation, spacing, texture, form, elevations, framing, light, and views from different angles.

Ultimately you want to create a strong composition that has both a defining character and a distinct relationship to the surrounding environment. Judicious use of ratios, spacing, orientation, quantity, and companion plantings will help you achieve that goal.

RATIOS

Ratios can help you determine the sizes of the stones you'll need to create a pleasing composition. If a composition has seven stones, assign the largest one a value of 100 percent. Two or three may be 65–75 percent of that; two or three others would be 30–45 percent of the largest stone; and one or two more would be 15–20 percent of it. Ratios are not absolute, but they serve as a sizing aid to use when you select stone for a composition. They yield the most information when used with other design tools, such as spacing and orientation.

SPACING

The amount of space between stones within a composition contributes to its wholeness or internal unity. Attention to spacing is also essential to create dynamic relationships between individual stones in the composition.

If stones are placed too far apart, they lose their connection to one another. If they're too close, their individual character is diminished. This holds true for purely sculptural compositions and for compositions that suggest or mimic natural features. In the latter, the care with which you space the stone also contributes to the authenticity of the composition. It should look like a grouping you might find in nature.

The relationship of stones to one another is an important design element.

USE PROPS. Spacing stone is a trial-and-error process that you can partially work out using a scale model or full-size cardboard shapes on the site. Large stone is cumbersome and expensive to move around, so make as many spacing decisions as you can before the actual installation.

ORIENTATION

As with spacing, orientation deals with the position of stones in relation to one another and with the overall integrity of the composition. To make decisions about orientation, evaluate what the faces and shape of each stone can contribute to the composition from all possible views. You may also play with the tilt or angle at which the stone is set.

QUANTITY

At some point during construction, you will have to make a decision about how many stones to use in a composition. Using 20 to 40 percent stone in a landscape is a general guide for projects of any scale. On the other hand, a Japanese-influenced composition could be 90 percent stone.

General recommendations are helpful, but it's still a challenge to know when to stop, even for a professional landscaper. Give yourself time for deliberation. Sometimes it can be helpful to add stones you're not sure about and then take them out later. Less is more if the composition seems complete with fewer stones. An odd number of stones is almost always easier to arrange than an even number.

▲ **The stone formation** the owners found on their property influenced this landscape design.

◄ **This grouping** of stone slabs, plants, and man-made elements forms a fascinating composition.

COMPANION PLANTINGS

If plants are part of your composition, include them in the plan drawings right from the start. This will help you avoid the disappointment of an arrangement with insufficient or too much space for plants. If you plan the space for plants at or near their mature size, you will minimize the amount of pruning needed to maintain the desired proportions of plant and stone.

If certain plants are essential to the overall composition, know the characteristics of the plants you choose for the site. If you need help with this part of the project, bring your drawing to a garden center to get assistance for choosing plants, or consult with a landscape designer.

Techniques and Tools

Once you know the size (approximate dimensions and weight) and shape (natural or dressed) of the stone you want to use, it will be easier to figure out what equipment will work best to set it. The most versatile piece of equipment to set large stone is an excavator with an articulating bucket and detachable thumb. It can excavate the site, replace subsoil with gravel, set and reposition stones, and backfill the site with topsoil and mulch material after the stones are in place.

SITE PREPARATION

Site preparation specific to setting large stone involves either digging holes to set the stones into or making level areas on which to set the stones. To make level areas, you may have to remove or add soil or gravel to create a stable spot at the right height. For long-term stability, always add fill in uniform layers.

CALCULATE STONE HEIGHT. If the height of individual stones is critical, try to get the height right the first time. It's especially cumbersome to raise stones, particularly if you're relying on hand tools to move them. (See "Setting Stone Height," opposite.)

The easiest way to get heights right in a stone composition is to use a transit and a fixed point from which to take readings. A low-tech method using string and stakes works, too. Use two or more stakes, depending on the configuration of your composition.

◀ **A line of striking stones** forms a pathway across an open field.

▶ **Take surface characteristics** into consideration when arranging stone in the landscape.

SETTING STONE HEIGHT

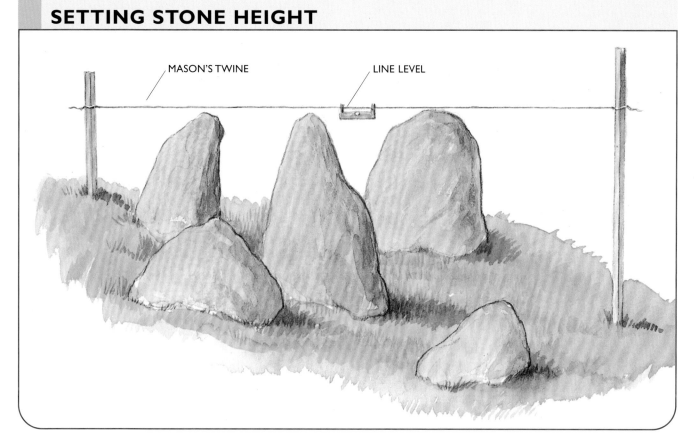

MASON'S TWINE

LINE LEVEL

JUDGING HEIGHT. Tie a piece of mason's line taut and level between the stakes at the height of the tallest stone. Measure down from this line to set shorter stones, or use additional stakes and lines. To set a stone at a specific height, you need to know the total height of the stone, the depth of the hole, and the amount of the stone that you want exposed above ground. This isn't so difficult on a relatively level site, but if the site is sloped, you may need disproportionately taller stones to get the effect you want.

DRAINAGE. Add drainage if your site is wet. The last thing you want is to have one or more stones in your composition list, or tip over, or to have the entire composition slowly slide down an incline.

PLACING STONES WITH HAND TOOLS

The series of illustrations below shows the various ways you can move a 100- to 300-pound stone into position with hand tools, depending on the specifics of the installation, site conditions, and your ingenuity. If you use

weight-rated tools like a come-a-long, you'll need to make some allowance for resistance if you pull stone along on the ground.

Keep small rocks handy to use as wedges. You'll use these to tweak the position of your stones and to hold stones in place until the backfilling is complete. Lengths of 2x4 or an iron bar are also handy for bracing stones temporarily.

COMBINE TECHNIQUES. In many instances, you will use a combination of techniques to get stone in place. For example, you may drag stone to the site with a chain and a truck from another location on your land. Then you may use a plank and rollers, a plank and pivot, or a come-a-long to get the stone next to the hole. To push the stone into position, you may "walk it" into place with pry bars, slide it on a plank, or push it with the bumper of your truck or a tractor bucket. In some instances, it may be easier to push a stone into a hole if one of the sides of the hole has been excavated to make an earthen ramp.

By now you're probably getting the idea that there's no

one way to work with large stone. It's true. But if you think through your options and experiment with unfamiliar tools, you'll figure out what works best for you.

PRY BAR. Pry bars are great for fine tuning stone placement. Use one or more pry bars to turn, tilt, or angle a stone into the desired position. A prybar can be used in combination with a fulcrum to increase your ability to tilt the stone. You can also use pry bars to walk a stone into position.

COME-A-LONG. There are two common situations for using a come-a-long. Use it in combination with a chain or harness of some sort to move stones short distances by dragging them along the ground. Or use it in combination with a tripod to lift a stone and set it into position.

PLANK AND ROLLERS. This was the method of choice to move the massive blocks used to build the pyramids. You can make rollers out of metal or PVC pipe or wood. They work best on even ground.

TRIPOD. A tripod is a three-legged support you make on-site and use in combination with a come-a-long, winch, chain-falls, or block and tackle. With this setup you can lower the stone into position and easily turn it to get it positioned. You can also easily raise the stone to add or remove fill.

CANT HOOK. A cant hook is a traditional logging tool used to roll and move logs. It also works well to move stone. With a cant hook, one person can grab, tilt, rotate, and roll a surprisingly large stone. The downside is you can't help but mar the stone if you use one. When you grab a stone, "hook" it in a place that will eventually be buried or concealed.

BALL CARTS. Garden centers and landscapers use ball

STONE-SETTING TECHNIQUES

Pry Bar

Plank and Rollers

Come-a-long

carts to move large plants. If this is a suitable way to move your stone, you may be able to rent one from a landscaper or garden center. Ball carts come in different sizes so match the load rating to the size of stones you want to move.

CHAIN OR ROPE. Use chain or rope to drag stones from one spot to another. Because there is a lot of resistance from the ground, use chain or rope rated for at least 2 times the estimated weight of your stone. You can move large stones with less drag, and less power, if you use a skid or plank and rollers in combination with the rope or chain. tool used to roll and move logs. It also works well to move stone. With a cant hook, one person can grab, tilt, rotate, and roll a surprisingly large stone. The downside is you can't help but mar the stone if you use one. When you grab a stone, "hook" it in a place that will eventually be buried or concealed.

BALL CARTS. Garden centers and landscapers use ball carts to move large plants. If this is a suitable way to move your stone, you may be able to rent one from a landscaper or garden center. Ball carts come in different sizes so match the load rating to the size of stones you want to move.

CHAIN OR ROPE. Use chain or rope to drag stones from one spot to another. Because there is a lot of resistance from the ground, use chain or rope rated for at least 2 times the estimated weight of your stone. You can move large stones with less drag, and less power, if you use a skid or plank and rollers in combination with the rope or chain.

ELECTRICAL TOOLS. Along with hand tools, there are a few electrical tools that could assist. For fitting and dressing large stones or large quantities, use an air hammer, a chipper, grinder, and power saw with abrasive blade.

Tripod

Cant Hook

SUPPORTING LARGE STONES

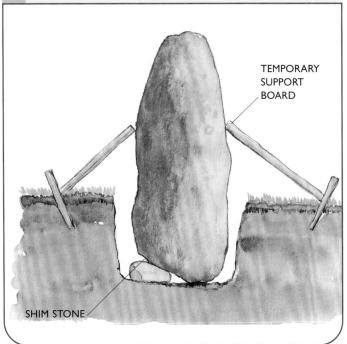

TEMPORARY SUPPORT BOARD

SHIM STONE

EARTHMOVING EQUIPMENT

To speed up the pace of the work or take it easy on your back, use an excavator, bulldozer, bobcat, or tractor to set stones that weigh more than 300 pounds. In the project shown on page 144, setting the stones that make the grade change took about 4 hours for a skilled operator and landscaper who often work together. The work proceeded quickly for this reason and because many of the stones and the fill materials were positioned within reach of the excavator bucket.

In that time they were able to install gravel fill (for drainage, stability, and proper elevation), set the stones, and distribute a 6-inch layer of topsoil over the area. Even the most skilled operator needs someone on the ground working with a shovel to either add or remove fill, position the stones, and even out the layers of fill and topsoil.

PROTECT THE STONE

It takes forethought to minimize the chipping, gouging, and scratching of the stone during an installation. You can reduce the amount of visible damage by identifying the exposed faces of the stone beforehand and then moving the stone in a way that protects the exposed faces. If you're using an excavator or bobcat, orient the stones so that the teeth don't come in contact with the good faces when you move the stone. Furniture-moving pads or blankets are sometimes useful to protect stone. While damage is unfortunate, most damage that occurs at installation will weather and blend in over time.

FINE-TUNE YOUR COMPOSITION. If possible, set each stone, but don't backfill for a day or two. This gives you time to discover and fix minor flaws before you finish the job. If that's not possible, try to take at least a few hours' break before final backfilling.

◄ **In this traditional** Japanese landscape design, horizontal stones are combined with plantings and man-made features.

► **Horizontal steps** were cut from the same stone as the surrounding boulders in this front-entry design.

WORKING WITH AN EQUIPMENT OPERATOR

BEFORE YOU CAN HIRE an equipment operator (or rent the equipment), you must determine exactly what it is you want to do and the general site layout. This will help the operator know which size and type of equipment is necessary to do the job. Have the following information at hand when you call a heavy-equipment operator:

▊ Number and size (approximate weight) of stones
▊ Buried services
▊ Water on the site
▊ Amount of space to maneuver equipment, or reach needed
▊ Topography of the site
▊ Site plan

▊ Timeline for project (During peak construction times, operators are sometimes booked months in advance. If your project is small and you can be flexible, sometimes they can work you into their schedule.)

Find an operator who has done this kind of work before and has a reputation for quality work. Garden centers and landscape designers should be able to provide you with names. Once you have selected one or two possible operators, check their references, and make an appointment for them to visit the site. Ideally, you want to hire an operator who enjoys this kind of work and is willing to work collaboratively with you. A skilled and reputable equipment operator can save you time and money.

9

SETTING ᴸARGE STONES

SETTING SPECIMEN STONES

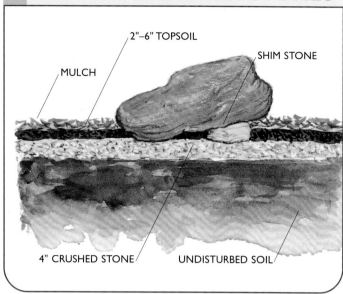

2"–6" TOPSOIL

MULCH

SHIM STONE

4" CRUSHED STONE

UNDISTURBED SOIL

BACKFILLING. Once you're satisfied with the composition, you can backfill. If you include large plants in your composition, you may want to set these as part of backfilling. The availability of equipment already on site can make moving and setting the plants easier.

SPECIMEN STONES

SPECIMEN STONES are placed in the landscape for aesthetic reasons and are not usually part of a functional garden feature. You can use a single specimen stone or arrange them in groups of 3, 5, 7, or more. Except for instances where absolute symmetry is required, it's easier to make a visually pleasing composition with odd numbers of stones. In this picture of an enclosed garden, the single large specimen stone is black with a rough-ridged surface that is uncommon in the area. However, because the garden is completely enclosed—its own world—a "foreign" stone does not seem out of place. Two smaller stones of the same geological type peek out from lush groundcover about 15 feet away from the large stone. Even though that distance would be too great in most compositions with stones this size, in this instance it's acceptable because the perimeter fence keeps the stones connected within the totality of the garden.

A variety of shrubs create an interesting counterpoint to this specimen stone.

MATCHING EQUIPMENT TO THE JOB

HERE'S THE TYPE OF EQUIPMENT you will need to move large stones. For this table, the size of stone is calculated at 160 pounds to the cubic foot. Always check with the earthmoving equipment company for capacity recommendations.

up to 300 lbs. or 2 cu. ft.	30–35 hp tractor w/bucket
up to 2,500 lbs. or 15.5 cu. ft.	60–80 hp tractor w/bucket
up to 2,000 lbs. or 12.5 cu. ft.	700 series bobcat
up to 4,000 lbs. or 25 cu. ft.	800 series bobcat
up to 10,000 lbs. or 62.5 cu. ft.	bulldozer, crane, or 29,000-lb. excavator

◄ **To create a natural look,** experiment with the placement of the stones.

▼ **The availability** of heavy equipment makes the use of large stones in the landscape possible.

Backfilling may include several layers of different materials. First use gravel or well-draining soil from the site to keep the stones stable. Leave enough room for 4 to 8 inches of topsoil, depending on your planting plans. On top of this, you may want to add several inches of bark mulch or crushed stone.

SAFETY. Safety is a concern on all landscape installations, but includes additional precautions when working with heavy equipment and big stone. Always maintain a safe distance from equipment. Use absolutely clear hand signals with the equipment operator. Stay in the operator's view. Restrict access to the site. Use equipment that is rated for the size stones with which you are working.

9

SETTING LARGE STONES

10

The popularity of less-formal gardens, Asian influences, and xeriscapes (landscaping that uses very little water) have stretched the definition of a 'Rock Garden' beyond its usual meaning. No longer is a rock garden strictly a mini re-creation of rugged terrain deliberately planted with tough alpine plants, sedums, and creeping phlox. Rock gardens have become sophisticated landscaping elements where natural stone plays as important a role as any of the selected plants.

ROCK
GARDENS

Choose a Site

Even with a more elastic definition, the beauty and charm of a rock garden depends on siting, choice and arrangement of the stones, and finding the right balance of vegetation and stone. If you keep these considerations in mind, you will be less constrained when selecting plants to use in the design. (See "Plants for Rock Gardens," pages 180–181.)

A natural rocky outcropping is nearly always the best choice for siting a rock garden, and often the outcropping is the inspiration for it. Adding other similar types of rock to create a garden can artfully expand even a small outcropping.

◄ **Brightly colored spring foliage** adds a pleasing contrast to the muted tones of the natural stone.

PLANT SELECTION. Traditional rock garden plants prefer sun. If you have a site that is partially or mostly shady, it will limit the variety of flowering plants that will bloom. However, there are many ferns, mosses, and woodland flowers that can be combined in a shady site for a striking rock garden. In shady sites, you need to evaluate how nearby large trees or shrubs will compete with your rock garden plants for water and nutrients. You will also want to consider whether leaves and plant litter will add an onerous maintenance chore.

Even with the most liberal interpretation, the essence of a rock garden is to mimic nature. Short of nature providing a choice site, look for a spot, preferably on a slope, where a rocky outcropping is plausible. If your space is limited, consider one or more container rock gardens or a small arrangement tucked away from formal elements, such as walkways, porches, and a clipped lawn.

10 ROCK GARDENS

Rock gardens offer the opportunity to introduce unique textures into the landscape.

Prepare the Site

The scale of your project and the presence of a natural stone outcropping will determine how much preparation your site will need. For constructed gardens, at the very least you will excavate holes to set the stones securely and at aesthetically pleasing angles. Remove sod as you would to make a new flowerbed. If the soil is heavy or needs drainage or if the stones may heave from freezing, remove and save the topsoil; then excavate down 4 to 12 inches below where the stones will set, and add gravel for drainage.

GARDENS IN WALLS

A rock garden wall is an alternative to a traditional rock garden. You might consider building one where there are space or topography limitations or where a wall would serve some other landscape design function.

SMART TIP

Container Rock Gardens

Container rock gardens offer a way to integrate a rock garden plant collection in a decidedly urban environment or in a more formal setting, such as an entryway or patio. If they are made portable, container rock gardens can be moved into a protected area in winter or out of the sun during the hottest weather.

► **Let natural formations,** such as this rock outcropping, serve as the foundation for your plants.

▼ **When selecting plants,** consider the type of soil and the amount of sun the area receives.

PLANT AS YOU BUILD. Typically, the plants are installed as the wall is built. To make the planting pockets in the wall, line the planting area with landscape fabric and partially fill the space with a soil mix suitable for the plant. Set the plant in place, and add as much additional soil as possible. Then gently tamp the soil, and water it thoroughly. You can cover the planted area with another piece of landscape fabric. If the planted area is not going to get covered with stone right away, cover the soil with wet burlap or mulch to protect the soil from drying out or being washed away.

Plants in walls are more vulnerable to weather extremes. Hand watering may be needed. To limit maintenance demands, you'll want to select plants for hardiness under extremely cold or dry conditions.

Sometimes a site can accommodate a stepped wall in a way that creates larger planting pockets. This can mean less demanding maintenance and allows you to use a wider variety of plants, including small shrubs.

Choose the Stone

When selecting stone for a rock garden or a garden wall, keep in mind that stone native to the area conveys belonging. On the other hand, you may want to use stone from another place to create a focal point.

Whatever your basis for choosing stone for a rock garden, its aesthetic value and structural importance are key to a successful project. The stones provide the frame, foundation, or skeleton—depending on how you look at it—of the garden. With your well thought-out planting plan in hand, arrange the stones to feature and complement your favorite plants.

NUMBER OF PLANTS. As with many landscaping decisions, there is no absolute ratio of stone to plants in a rock garden. One-third stone and two-thirds plants is a commonly cited ratio. In reality your site, maintenance demands, and personal preferences can easily stretch the range from as little as 20 percent to 60 percent stone.

PLANTING A DRY-LAID WALL

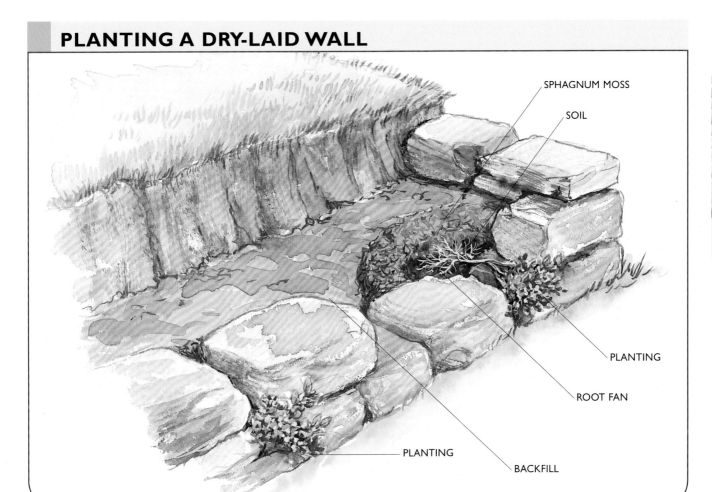

SPHAGNUM MOSS

SOIL

PLANTING

ROOT FAN

PLANTING

BACKFILL

◄ **A grouping of stone** on a level area forms an island in the landscape.

► **Pond kits and liners** make it easy to include a water feature as a complement to your rock garden.

When selecting plants, take their growing patterns and size at maturity into consideration.

Arrange the Stone

When it comes to arranging the stones in a rock garden, there is general agreement on some basic design principles. The first: let nature be your teacher.

▌ Use one kind of stone. However, in large gardens you may introduce a different kind of stone as a special feature.

▌ If you use crushed stone mulch, try to match the color of it to the dominant stone used in the garden.

▌ Use sun and prevailing wind exposure to set stones in a way that creates microclimates.

▌ Bury at least one-half of each stone or up to the stone's widest part. You'll want the stones to look settled into the ground, not sitting on top of it.

▌ Arrange the stones so that grain, striations, or fracture lines are all pointed in the same direction.

▌ Use stones of various sizes, placing the largest at the top of the garden.

After you have arranged all the stones, study your composition for a few days or longer. If possible, set key plants where you plan to plant them. Now is the time to make changes in your composition. After the stones are set, redistribute the topsoil around the stones and make pockets of special soil mixes for specific plants.

SMART TIP

Future Planning

If you plant your rock garden over a number of years, place pieces of plastic covered with mulch over future planting areas. This will reduce the amount of weed seed that can germinate.

▲ **Combining the right stone** with the right plant can create pockets of surprise in your rock garden.

▼ **A bowl** filled with coins combined with a variety of rocks and native plants makes an interesting focal point.

WATER IN A ROCK GARDEN

ADDING MOVING WATER to a rock garden where it is not naturally present adds a level of complexity to the project. However, adding a feature that contains still water is a much easier task. Sometimes you can find a stone with a hollow spot in it, making a natural basin for a small reflecting pool. Clay pots, stone bowls, and metal cans sunk in the ground and painted black can all make satisfactory reflecting pools. You can also make shallow free-form shapes using plastic pond liner material.

PLANTS FOR ROCK GARDENS

Name	Common	Zone	Ht.	Bloom	Color	Notes
Grasses						
Carex humilis	**Blue sedge**	5–9	6"–8"	Late summer	Tawny	Good ground cover in rock gardens; holds soil; forms clumps.
Festuca cinerea	**Blue fescue**	4–8	10"	Late summer	Blue foliage	Tufting; fruiting heads reach 2' tall; good with succulents.
Dwarf Conifers						
Chamaecyparis obtusa 'Nana'	**Dwarf Hinoki cypress**	4–8	1.5'	n/a	Dark green	Grows only 20" wide; leaves look like thick moss.
Juniperus communis 'Echiniformis'	**Hedgehog juniper**	2–7	2'	n/a	Clear green	The hummock-like shape adds needed contrast to a rock garden.
J. chinensis	**Sargent juniper**	4–9	2'–3'	n/a	Blue green	Adds color and shape to a rock garden.
J. squamata	**Singleseed juniper**	4–7	2'–3'	n/a	Silver green	Provides contrast for other plants.

Sargent juniper 'Sargentii'

Singleseed juniper 'Blue Star'

Name	Common	Zone	Ht.	Bloom	Color	Notes
Shrubs						
Calluna vulgaris	**Heather**	4–7	2.5'	Winter to spring	Range	Choose dwarf heathers; heather requires acid (6–5.5) pH soil.
Erica carnea	**Winter or spring heath**	4–7	1'	Winter to spring	White, pink, red, purple	Many cultivars are available; heath requires alkaline soil.
Rhododendron impeditum	**Yunan rhododendron**	6–8	1.5'	Spring	Purplish-blue	This dwarf shrub has tiny leaves in scale with its size.

Heather 'Corbett Red'

Scotch Heather

Scotch Heather 'Blazeaway'

Heath 'Springwood White'

Heath 'Vivelli'

Name	Common	Zone	Ht.	Bloom	Color	Notes
Perennials						
Achillea clavennae	**Silver alpine yarrow**	3–7	1'	Late spring	White	Requires alkaline (7.5) soil.
Aquilegia canadensis	**Rock columbine**	3–8	1'	Late spring	Red, yellow	Requires alkaline to neutral soil; tolerates light shade.
Aquilegia saximontana	**Colorado columbine**	4–6	4"	Spring	Blue, yellow	Requires neutral soil and a sunny location.
Arabis spp.	**Rockcress, Wallcress**	4–7	4"–1.5'	Summer	White	Requires alkaline-to-neutral soil in sunny location; many species are available.
Armeria caespitosa, A. maritima	**Thrift**	5–8	4"–8"	Early summer	Pink, white	Requires neutral soils in a sunny location; excellent cut flower, too.
Gentiana spp.	**Gentian**	3–7	2"–1.5'	Summer to fall	Blue	Several species are available; prefers sunny location.
Leontopodium alpinum	**Edelweiss**	5–7	4"–6"	Late spring-summer	Yellowish-gray/white	This traditional alpine plant requires alkaline soils in sunny locations.
Penstemon spp.	**Penstemon**	Range	Range	Spring to summer	Blue, red pink, white	Wide choice of species, cultivars; some tolerate acid soils and partial shade.
Sedum spp.	**Sedum**	Range	Range	Summer	Pink, red, yellow	Many species and cultivars are suitable.
Thymus spp.	**Thyme**	Range	Range	Late spring, summer	Pink, purple	Choose creeping species such as *T. serpyllum* & *T. pseudolanuginosus*.
Veronica prostrata	**Cliff speedwell**	5–7	6"–8"	Summer	Blue, white	Place in full sun with neutral pH soil.
Veronica spicata	**Alpine speedwell**	3–7	6"–8"	Summer	Blue, white	Place in full sun with neutral pH soil.

Armeria maritima Thrift

Penstemon 'Australis'

Penstemon 'Beard Tongue'

Sedum 'Autumn Joy'

Sedum

Alpine speedwell

Penstemon 'Coccineus'

11

Stone walls remain popular landscape features, even if they are no longer used to confine livestock or protect gardens. A length of stone wall along the border of a garden or yard is an enduring reminder of the past, yet it is compatible with contemporary designs and lifestyles. In urban and suburban areas, you can use stone walls to establish property lines, create privacy, convey a feeling of security, define an outdoor room, or complement the rest of the landscape design.

FREESTANDING
WALLS

Creating Stone Walls

There are two types of freestanding walls, dry-laid and mortared. In dry-laid stone walls, the individual stones are stacked one on top of the other without being held together with mortar, creating an informal, casual structure. This is the type of wall associated with the New England countryside, although such a wall constructed of local stone will fit anywhere.

Mortared stone walls are more formal in appearance. Bonding the stones together with mortar adds stability to the walls, but they are generally more difficult to build.

USES FOR STONE WALLS. With two exposed sides, a freestanding wall often does double duty in a home landscape. Viewed from the outside, a stone wall defines a boundary and adds texture to the landscape. The use of local stone helps to integrate the entire landscape design. When viewed from inside a landscape, a stone wall not only defines the boundary of a garden or the entire property but also serves as a backdrop for other landscape features.

▲ **A traditional-looking wall** marks the boundaries of a yard. The wall shown here is made from native stone.

▶ **A sturdy flagstone wall** partially encloses this elevated patio area.

From inside the garden, the stone wall shown on the bottom left on the opposite page is an enclosure that adds intimacy, defines a garden area, and complements the plants in the garden. Outside the garden, the wall indicates the edge of the orchard adjacent to the garden. Interestingly, the decision to build the wall was borne of an unrelated necessity—what to do with mountains of rock produced from blasting for a building foundation. The owner's decision-making process is reminiscent of an earlier time when walls were created from the stones farmers cleared from their fields.

STONE FOR YOUR WALL

There are many types of stone you can use to build free-standing walls. Quarried limestone, sandstone, and slate are easy to work but not always available. Round stone or field rubble is the most difficult (some would say impossible) to use to build a stable freestanding wall, especially a dry-laid stone wall. Uniform rectilinear stone is generally more expensive and makes a more formal wall, but it is faster to lay up and an easier material with which to work.

SORTING THE STONE. Unlike building a patio or walkway, you can't lay out the entire stone wall ahead of time to make aesthetic decisions about individual stones. What you can do is get to know your stone by sorting it. Set aside stones for specific purposes: the largest, flattest stones for the base course, the squarest for the ends of the

◄ **A mortared wall** such as this one requires a concrete footing for stability.

▼ **A wall made of** dressed stone requires less mortar than one made of field stone.

SMART TIP

Delivery Pointer
If stone is delivered on pallets, have the driver set them along the length of the wall to reduce handling on your part.

wall, bond stones to span wythes, thinner flat stones for capstones, wall stones of varying sizes, and rubble to fill in between the wythes. As you sort the stone, try to visualize how you will mix the various sizes in the wall. Will you set distinctive stones in a way that contributes to a rhythm for the wall? You may want to practice laying up a section of wall to find such a rhythm.

TRAIN YOUR EYE. The most important skills you need to build a sturdy and visually pleasing wall come with practice. You want to be able to select stone that fits both structurally and aesthetically in a given space, and you want to be able to make spaces to use the stones you have. Knowing your stone allows you to use both of these approaches to build your wall.

11

FREESTANDING WALLS

Dry-Laid Freestanding Walls

The width of a wall depends on the wall's finished height. The base of a freestanding wall is generally one-half to two-thirds of the height. Because the stone pattern will be more random, you'll want a wider base if you're working with fieldstone rather than with semidressed or dressed stone.

Freestanding walls are usually two wythes wide, meaning that most of the stones used are only half as wide as the wall. This allows you to angle the stones toward the middle of the wall to increase the strength and durability of the wall.

BUILDING BASICS

Dry-laid walls can flex with the movement of the earth, so they do not require a concrete footing. The walls rest directly on level soil—a 6-inch-deep trench is all you need to begin building. But if the soil drains poorly or is sandy, excavate an additional 6 to 12 inches and backfill the trench to within 6 inches of the grade with compacted gravel. You get the best results if you add the gravel in 2-inch layers, compacting as you go.

AN EXCEPTION TO THE RULE. Driveways and walkways that are cleared of snow tend to have a deeper frost line than areas that remain snow covered. If the wall abuts a plowed driveway or walkway, minimize damage

DRY-LAID STONE WALL CONSTRUCTION

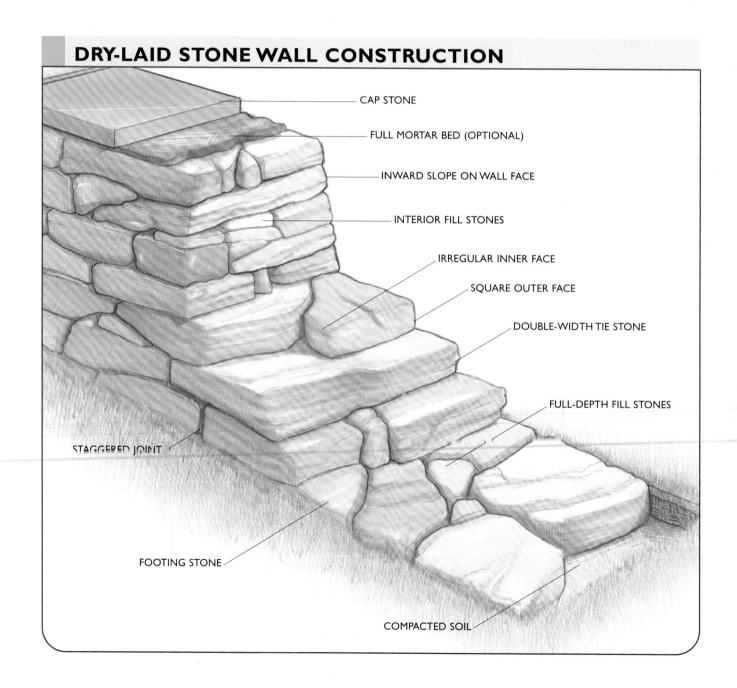

CAP STONE

FULL MORTAR BED (OPTIONAL)

INWARD SLOPE ON WALL FACE

INTERIOR FILL STONES

IRREGULAR INNER FACE

SQUARE OUTER FACE

DOUBLE-WIDTH TIE STONE

FULL-DEPTH FILL STONES

STAGGERED JOINT

FOOTING STONE

COMPACTED SOIL

caused by soil heaving by installing a concrete footing below the frost line. Of course, dry-laid stone walls are easy to repair, and a small amount of damage should not be a problem. Consult local building officials as to the need for dry-laid wall footings.

A low dry-laid wall defines the border of a garden. When building, install both wythes at the same time.

SMART TIP

Picking Capstones
Select your capstones, and set them aside until you are ready to finish the top of the wall. The top is the most important face of a wall.

Sort stones into categories before you start building.

CONSTRUCTION TIP

Stake Out the Wall

Use stakes and string to outline the base of the wall. If you will be laying stone in courses, level the lines a few inches above the height of the first course. Then measure down from the line to check your courses for level. Adjust the strings as you add more courses to the wall.

These cap stones were set perpendicular to the other stones.

TYPES OF STONE. Use the largest, flattest stones for the first course, and set them with the flattest side up. Bond stones are double-wide stones that span the entire width or both wythes of the wall; they help tie the wall together as a structure. Place bond stones at either end of the wall and every 4 to 6 feet along the length of the wall. (See "Dry-Laid Stone Wall Construction," page 188.)

As you place the stones, cant them toward the middle of the wall. This means the vertical surface of the wall will recede slightly with each course. This is called the batter. Ideally, a stone wall should have a ½- to 1-inch batter per vertical foot of height. Canting the stones in this way makes the wall more stable. You can build a wall with plumb

vertical faces if you are building with dressed stone and the wall is less than 2 feet tall. (See "Make a Batter Gauge," page 205.)

It's easier to fit the stones together if you work your way down the length of the wall installing both wythes at the same time rather than installing one wythe and then going back to install the other.

After the main wall stones are set, go back and fill in between them with smaller stones. Pack the rubble between the wythes as tightly as you can without dislodging the wall stones.

THE OTHER COURSES. As you set each course on the wall, chisel or knock off projections on the stones to improve the fit and to seat the stones firmly. You can also use small wedge-shaped pieces of stone to prevent the wall stones from rocking. When you use stone wedges this way, set them deep in the wall where they are less likely to get knocked out of place.

Place stones to straddle the joints created by the stones below them: either one stone over two, or two over one. This technique, in addition to bond stones, batter, and canting the stones, contributes to the overall stability and integrity of the wall.

Cap stones should overhang the edges of the rest of the wall. Stagger joints between the courses for strength.

FINISHING THE WALL. The top courses are installed in the same way. If you have a limited number of suitable bond stones, set them in every other course. If a wall turns a corner, overlap bond stones to make the corner and connect the two walls.

As you work along, you can fill large gaps between wall stones with smaller stones. Use a hammer to tap the stones into place without displacing the wall stones.

CAP STONES. When you lay the top course, try to make it as flat and level as possible so the cap stones won't wobble.

Typically, the flattest, best-looking stones are used to cap the wall. The cap stones are generally set to overhang the rest of the wall. You can mortar the cap stones in place if they are not large and if the wall will be used as seating.

Mortaring the cap stones also reduces the amount of water that gets into the wall. This protects the wall from heaving in the event of a wet fall followed by freezing temperatures before there is much snow cover.

In milder climates you can use a 2- to 4-inch-thick mortar cap. Tilt or crown the mortar cap at least ⅛ inch per foot so that it sheds water.

▼ **Uniform, square-cut stone** is easier to work with than field rubble, but it is more expensive.

▼ **A low garden wall** such as this one is often used as a backdrop for plantings.

A FREESTANDING PLANTING BED

WITH A FEW MODIFICATIONS you can make a planting bed in a freestanding wall. As a general guideline you would replace the rubble between the two wythes with high-quality soil suitable for the plants you intend to grow there. Do not reduce or eliminate the bond stones that tie the two wythes together. To hold the soil in place, install a layer of landscape fabric between the soil and the wall stones. Cut and overlap the landscape fabric to fit it around the bond stones.

Freestanding walls are one way to make gardening more accessible. A bed can be made high enough to garden from a sitting or standing position.

As with planting a retaining wall, a planting bed in a freestanding wall is a stressful environment for plants. (See "Gardens in Walls," page 174.) Plants that would survive in the ground might freeze in a freestanding planting bed. In a hot, sunny location, the maintenance watering might make planting in a freestanding wall impractical.

Mortared Freestanding Walls

A mortared stone wall gives you more flexibility for siting a wall than does a dry-laid wall. Because of the mortar between courses and a concrete footing, mortared walls can be tall yet relatively narrow.

Because mortared walls can be built narrower, they are often preferred where space is limited. You may also want to consider mortaring a wall that will do double duty as seating or is in a living and entertainment area where a wall is apt to get leaned upon.

Mortared walls less than 4 feet tall are feasible for a homeowner with little or no experience. Like dry-laid walls, the more dressed or uniform the stone, the quicker the wall will go up. A mortared wall is more formal than a dry-laid wall and more expensive to build in cold climates.

MORTARED STONE WALL CONSTRUCTION

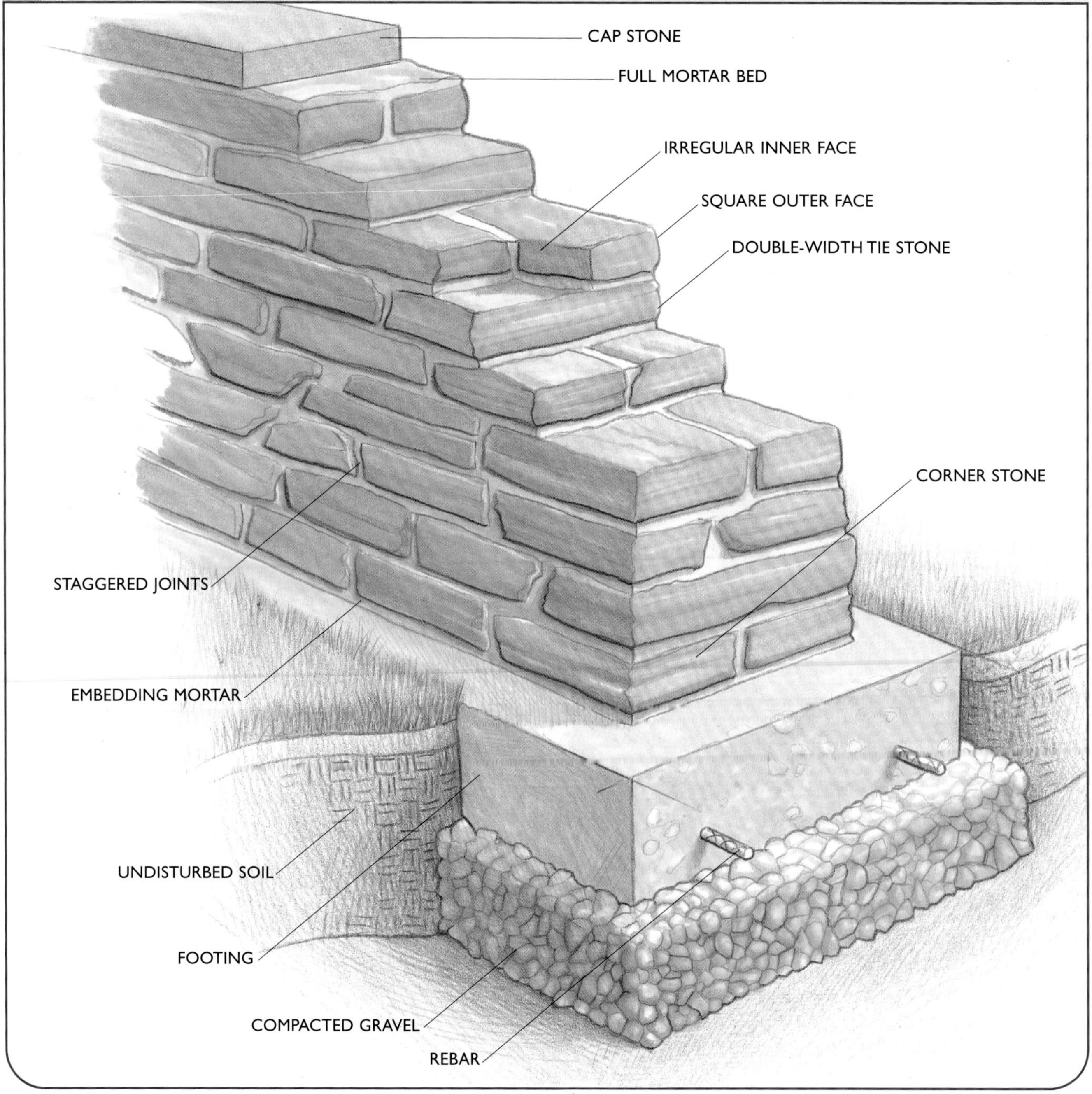

- CAP STONE
- FULL MORTAR BED
- IRREGULAR INNER FACE
- SQUARE OUTER FACE
- DOUBLE-WIDTH TIE STONE
- CORNER STONE
- STAGGERED JOINTS
- EMBEDDING MORTAR
- UNDISTURBED SOIL
- FOOTING
- COMPACTED GRAVEL
- REBAR

Estimate mortar needs by building a section of wall and then multiplying by the number of sections.

CONCRETE FOOTINGS. Because a mortared wall cannot flex with the movement of the earth, it needs a concrete footing. Typically the footing is twice the width of the wall and as deep as the wall is wide. For example, a 14-inch-thick wall would have a 28-inch-wide footing that is 14 inches thick. In cold climates, a footing must extend below the frost line to keep a wall from heaving. Once your footing is in place, building a mortared wall is similar to building a dry-laid wall.

MORTARED WALL DRAINAGE

Mortared walls can cause pooling of rainwater after storms. In areas where occasional heavy rain events occur, consider installing a perforated drain pipe below grade along the uphill side of the wall or building daylight drain holes through the wall, which allows free flow of water and prevents flooding.

WORKING WITH MORTAR

The amount of mortar you need depends on the type of stone you use and the size of joints in the wall. A fieldstone wall will use more mortar than one built with dressed stone. To calculate how much mortar you'll need, first build a section of wall, keeping track of how much mortar you use. Multiply that amount by the number of sections of wall remaining. For example, if you build a 5-foot section and your wall is 20 feet long, you will need three times the amount you used in the first section to finish the wall. (20 divided by 5 equals 4, and one section is already complete).

If you are building with rough quarry stone or fieldstone, test-fit your stone first. Then remove the stone; make a 1- to 2-inch-thick mortar bed; and set the stone.

After one or two courses (6 to 10 inches) of wall stones are laid, pack the space between the wythes with a mixture of rubble and concrete. If you are building in courses with dressed stone, you can build up the ends of the wall after laying the first course. This helps keep the wall level, plumb, and square.

11

FREESTANDING WALLS

FOOTING CONSTRUCTION

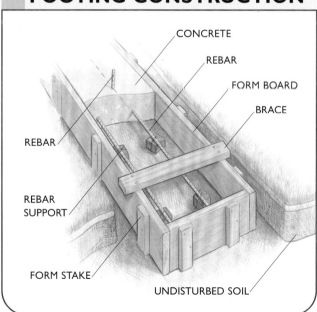

CONCRETE

REBAR

FORM BOARD

BRACE

REBAR

REBAR SUPPORT

FORM STAKE

UNDISTURBED SOIL

FILLING IN THE SPACES. After the stones in each course are set in mortar, fill the spaces between the stones. The easiest way to get mortar into the joints is to first load some mortar on your trowel; then with a quick downward motion, fling the mortar into the joint. Clean up the joints by removing excess mortar using your trowel. Follow by using a wet sponge to wipe off mortar that gets on the face of the stone. Remove this mortar as soon as possible.

TOOLING THE JOINTS. Smooth the mortar joints with a mason's jointing tool, a piece of wood with the end rounded, or a round-headed bolt sized for your joints. The tooled joints help shed water, and they contribute to the overall look of the finished wall. There are a variety of options here, so study other stonework to see which type of joint you like best. It is possible to mortar a wall built with fieldstone or semidressed stone so that to the casual observer the mortar doesn't show.

TIME FOR TOOLING. When you tool the joints is more critical than how. Test the mortar by pushing your thumb into it. When the mortar is firm but you can still leave an imprint, the mortar is ready for tooling. The amount of time it takes for the mortar to get to this stage varies with temperature, humidity, and sun and wind exposure. Cover sections of wall with wet burlap to slow down the drying time. Setting a timer as a reminder to check the mortar is helpful, especially when you are still establishing a routine for laying up stone, filling joints, and tooling them.

Use a whisk broom to remove loose bits of mortar and smooth out the surface of the joints. If needed, use a wire brush to remove any mortar that may still be stuck to the stones. **CAUTION:** soft stone, such as sandstone, could become marred from excessive brushing. Test a piece of stone before using a wire brush on it.

▲ **Tooled joints** look better on a mortar wall, and they help the wall shed water.

CONSTRUCTION TIP

Setting Large Stones

If you are setting a large stone, you may need to use wedges to hold the stone in place until the mortar sets up. Scrape off excess mortar that squeezes out with the edge of your trowel.

► **Although recently constructed,** this stone and metal wall looks as if it has been in place a long time.

▼ **Experiment with the stone** you have to determine the best location for each piece.

12

Retaining walls let you alter the grade or slope of the land to create level areas that you can use for planting, adding a patio, or any one of a number of uses. They also protect the slope from eroding or collapsing. As with freestanding stone walls, you can build a dry-laid wall or a mortared version. Dry-laid walls are informal and do not require a concrete footing, so they are easier to build than mortared retaining walls. Mortared walls offer more stability, but they tend to be more difficult to build.

RETAINING
WALLS

Retaining-Wall Designs

The featured project below illustrates some of the other benefits of building stone retaining walls. By adding a wall to an uninspired level lawn, this homeowner achieved several goals. She created a sunken garden room that proves an asset to her bed-and-breakfast business, and it allows her to indulge her passion for gardening. Because stone holds heat, the growing beds in the garden room extend the harvest season and accelerate plant growth without protective covers. The heat-trapping effect of the design also extends the season for using the area as an outdoor sitting room.

The walls in the sunken garden of this ambitious project are a good example of retaining wall construction. With thoughtful, creative planning you can build a dry-laid retaining wall that is handsome, durable, and an asset to your landscape.

Retaining walls create a sunken garden room that extends the normal growing season.

PREPARING THE SITE

Begin by calculating the height of the wall. Usually, the angle of the slope determines the height of the wall—the steeper the slope the taller the wall. There are exceptions to this rule. For example, privacy walls are usually tall no matter how steep the slope against which they are built. You may want a wall at a specific height so that you can get access to a garden bed.

Tall walls are more difficult and more costly to build. Structural and drainage issues are more critical for walls more than 3 feet tall and, if you have no prior experience, should not be attempted without professional advice or assistance. The visual mass of a tall wall can also present problems. Rather than build one tall wall, consider adding terraces and building a series of shorter walls.

◀ **As with freestanding walls,** flat, square-cut stone is the easiest with which to work.

▼ **Use retaining walls** to create level areas for planting. The height of some parts of the wall makes it easy to tend to the plants shown.

12 RETAINING WALLS

TERRACING A SLOPE. Farmers have been terracing hillsides for thousands of years. For a homeowner, the incentive usually comes from a desire to turn an otherwise uninspiring or difficult-to-maintain hillside into accessible and attractive gardens.

The shorter walls typical of terraces require less skill to fabricate, and you can construct them in stages. Terraces are also less expensive to construct than one tall wall, and they create an inviting destination. All the steps that apply to retaining walls apply to terracing a natural hillside or constructed berm. If the slope is steep and you want wide terraces, then you will have extra fill to remove from the site.

EXCAVATION. Once you know the location and height of the wall, you are ready to begin excavating the site. Short walls with little slope behind them may require nothing more than removing the sod and excavating down 4 to 6 inches. On sloped ground, excavation is usually a cut-and-fill process. As you cut into the slope, you use the soil to level off another area.

Plan on excavating more soil than may appear necessary. You will need space for the wall, space to work, room for gravel backfill, and space for additional backfill to minimize pressure on the wall—an important consideration for walls that front steep, tall slopes.

In many cases, you will end up with more soil than you can use on the current project. Try to find some other landscaping use for the removed soil.

THE BASE OF THE WALL. Because they can shift with the movement of the earth, dry-laid retaining walls do not require a concrete footing. In gravelly soil that drains well, remove the sod and 4 to 6 inches of topsoil. Slope the grade in the trench ¼ to ½ inch per foot into the hill. In sandy or wet soils, excavate an additional 4 to 12 inches; lay down landscape fabric; and backfill the trench with gravel that compacts and drains.

If you are unsure, overbuild. If you think it may be necessary, increase the depth of the gravel base and install drain pipe to prevent the wall toppling in an intense storm.

SMART TIP

Walls and Permits

Before you start digging, find out whether you need a permit to build a dry-laid stone retaining wall.

RETAINING-WALL CONSTRUCTION

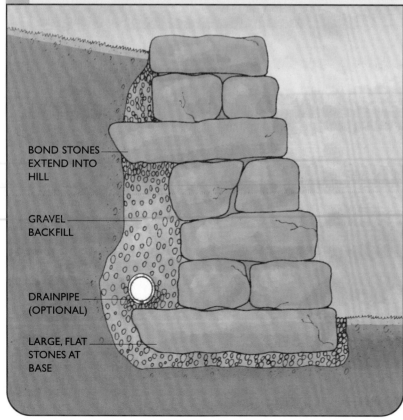

BOND STONES EXTEND INTO HILL

GRAVEL BACKFILL

DRAINPIPE (OPTIONAL)

LARGE, FLAT STONES AT BASE

▲ **This dramatic retaining wall** provides a planting area for brightly colored shrubs and flowers.

◀ **Building with rounded stone** is challenging and best used on short walls.

The height of the wall will determine the width of your trench. Use this guide: for walls under 3 feet tall, make the width of the wall at its base equal to one-half the finished height of the wall; for taller walls, the width of the base should be closer to two-thirds the height of the wall. A 3-foot-tall wall should have a 2-foot-wide base. Consult a professional mason or landscape contractor when planning on a wall that is taller than 3 feet.

Mortared walls require a concrete footing. Local building codes determine the depth and width of the footing.

▲ **To facilitate drainage** as you set the stones, backfill with gravel behind the wall.

CONSTRUCTION TIP

Make a Batter Gauge

Stone walls should slope inward from bottom to top. To check the inward slope as you build, construct a batter gauge from 1x2s joined at one end and spread apart at the other. **1.** The distance between the two ends is the slope you want to maintain. To use the gauge, hold the sloping 1x2 against the wall, and place a level on the other board. **2.** You are maintaining the right amount of batter when the level reads plumb.

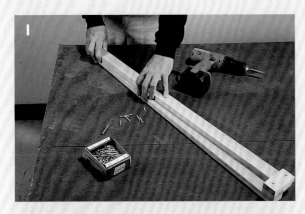

◀ **Instead of a single high wall,** consider building a series of stepped layers that you can then plant.

▶ **Runoff from the slope** will seep out between the stones of a dry-laid retaining wall.

DRAINAGE. Runoff from the slope will seep out between the stones of a dry-laid retaining wall. Typically, these types of walls do not require an additional drainage system. But if the site is wet and you want to minimize seepage through the wall, add a drainpipe that can move the water away from the wall. Backfilling with a few inches of coarse gravel minimizes erosion and loss of soil through the wall. For greater stability, particularly with steep slopes, lay landscape fabric between the soil and the backfill gravel.

If you are planning a mortared wall, you must provide a drainage system. Without weep holes or some other drainage system, runoff from the slope will exert tremendous pressure against the wall, resulting in buckling of the wall.

BUILDING THE WALL

When the stone is delivered to the site, sort it as you would for a freestanding wall: larger stones for the base, bond stones to span between wythes, rubble for fill between the wythes, and cap stones or coping for the top of the wall. Unlike freestanding walls, retaining walls need only one good face. If your wall is short and there isn't a lot of pressure on it, you can build the wall one stone wide provided your stones are large and good building stone, that is, they fit together well.

CALCULATE THE BATTER. Retaining walls lean back into the slope they support. This lean is called the batter. Retaining walls typically have about a 2-inch batter for every foot of height. If a wall is short and the stone is at least semidressed, you can reduce or eliminate the batter.

LAY THE BASE COURSE. Use your largest and flattest stones for the base course. Place bond stones at each end of the wall and at 4- to 6-foot intervals along the wall. Ideally, the bond stones should be long enough to extend into the slope. Between the bond stones, lay wall stones, one in front of the other, to create a double-wythe wall. Fill any gaps between these stones with smaller stones or rubble.

Tilt all the main wall stones into the hill. After laying the first course, you can backfill along the front of the wall and firmly tamp the soil in 2-inch layers. If you are going to install perforated drainpipe, now is the time to lay it along the backside of the wall. Slope the pipe to facilitate drainage.

ADD THE REMAINING COURSES. Place the next course, setting it back slightly from the first. Stagger the location of the bond stones, offsetting them from the bond stones in the first course. Lay stones so that all joints between courses are staggered.

After the second course is laid, backfill with gravel and fill almost to the top of the second course. Firmly tamp the gravel in 2-inch layers. Continue laying up courses in the same manner, checking the angle of the face with your batter gauge periodically and backfilling after every two courses.

CAP THE WALL. Cap stones usually span the width of the wall and protrude slightly over it. Because water can move through a dry-laid wall, the water-shedding function of the cap stones isn't as crucial. For stability, especially if the wall is located somewhere where it will be used as seating, you may want to mortar the capstones.

FINISH BACKFILLING AND GRADING. After laying the capstones, backfill with gravel up to within 4 inches or so of the top of the wall. Lay landscape fabric over the top of the gravel, and finish backfilling with soil or mulch.

▶ **Retaining walls** lean back into the slope. Plan on a 2-in. batter for every foot of height.

▼ **Lay retaining wall stones** so that all joints between courses are staggered.

This charming water feature is enclosed by an informal-looking stone retaining wall.

FIRE PIT CONSTRUCTION

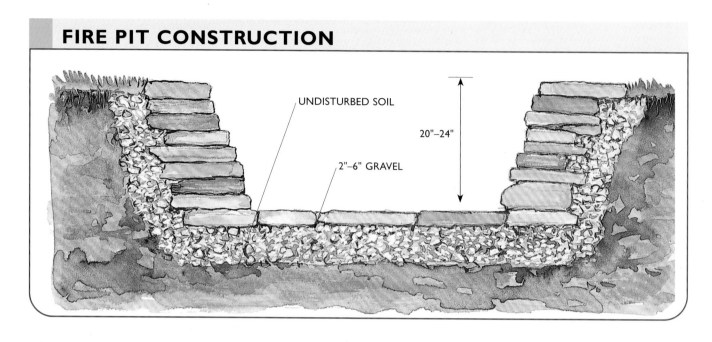

UNDISTURBED SOIL

2"–6" GRAVEL

20"–24"

Adding a Fire Pit

Using the same techniques for building a retaining or freestanding wall, you can build a stone fire pit in an outdoor living area to add a welcoming gathering spot to your landscape. A fire pit reduces the effects of wind on a fire, and for serious stargazers it has the added benefit of containing the fire glow.

LOCATING THE FIRE PIT. Likely locations for a fire pit include in the backyard; adjacent to a patio; on a beach; or by a pond or pool. You can build a fire pit on a hillside, but you will have to level an area first. Ultimately, the absence of fire hazards will determine potential locations for a fire pit. Choose a site that is a safe distance from buildings, fuel storage, and supply lines, and from overhanging tree branches and utility wires. Beyond this, and the general site considerations in Chapter Two, build your fire pit with leisure and entertaining in mind.

SIZE THE FIRE PIT. There are no hard-and-fast rules for fire-pit proportions. A tapered pit is more engaging visually, especially if the pit is less than 5 feet in diameter. Whatever the size, you need a hole 24 to 36 inches wider than the desired finished inside dimensions. For a 36- to 42-inch-wide by 20- to 24-inch-deep pit, excavate a 6-foot-diameter hole.

The depth of the hole depends on the thickness of the bottom stone(s), the type of soil, and the desired finished depth of the pit. To calculate hole depth, add up the finished depth of the pit, the thickness of the bottom stone, and the thickness of the gravel base.

EXCAVATE THE HOLE. Outline the perimeter of the fire pit with a garden hose or string. If you have to remove sod, use a digging spade to cut it up. Cut through the sod around the perimeter of the hole; then cut the sod into manageable pieces. Use it to patch bare spots elsewhere, or compost it. Excavate the topsoil separately, and save it for grading afterwards.

After you excavate the hole, level the bottom. Check for level using a 4-foot carpenter's level, a straight 4-foot board, or a 2x4 on edge with a 2-foot level on top. Tamp the bottom of the hole firmly; then add at least 2 inches of gravel that compacts but also drains. In heavy soils or

where there is seasonal standing water or below freezing temperatures, use up to 8 inches of gravel and tamp it in 2-inch layers.

BUILD THE FIRE PIT

To build a fire pit, you will set dry-laid stone in a cone shape. To build in the round, try to use stones with one side longer than the other. If you don't spend a lot of time shaping the stones, the wall will look good from above but can have wedge-shaped gaps between some of the stones. Fill these spaces with small nonload-bearing stones. In other words, as you build, keep the load on the wall stones as in traditional stone-wall construction.

LAY THE FIRST COURSE. To begin, set the stone or stones that form the bottom of the pit in the middle of the hole. Then set the first course of stones around the bottom stone. It's okay if there are gaps between the bottom and wall stones.

CALCULATE THE SETBACK. To build a tapered pit, you need to calculate the setback for each course. To do this, first estimate the number of courses it will take to build the pit. To calculate the setback for each course, take ½ of the difference between the bottom and top finished diameters of the pit and divide by the number of courses. For example, for a pit 24 inches wide at the bottom and 36 inches wide at the top, the difference is 12 (36 minus 24). One-half of the difference between those two measurements is 6. If there are eight courses, divide 6 by 8, which gives you 0.75 or ¾ of an inch. In this example, each course is set back ¾ inch from the one below it.

◄ **A fire pit** will become a destination in your landscape design.

► **Choose a site** for your fire pit that is a safe distance from buildings, fuel storage, and utility wires.

ADD BACKFILL. Begin backfilling after you lay up about 6 inches of wall. Compact the backfill using a hoe, tamper, or your feet. Water the area. Repeat this process after building each successive 6 inches of wall. Some backfill will work its way through the wall over time. In other walls, landscape fabric is used to keep backfill from migrating into the stonework. In this application, the heat from the fire could eventually melt the fabric or char natural fiber burlap. You could use metal screen in place of weed-barrier fabric. Or use small rocks or crushed stone for a few inches behind the wall stones; then fill in the remaining space with some of the excavated soil. If the excavated soil is heavy clay, backfill with gravel.

CAP THE PIT. When the construction is within two courses of the surrounding grade, take some rough measurements so that the fire pit surround stones end up at the level you want and can be set on a 1-inch-per-foot slope away from the pit. After you set each of the stones that edge the pit, do a safety check. Ask someone who weighs at least 150 pounds to stand on the stone and lean out over the pit as far as possible without falling in. Repeat this for each stone that edges the pit. If a stone tips up even the slightest bit, reset it or replace it. Once the construction is complete, you may have to cut or fill to make a transition from the excavation area to the surrounding grade. The photos shown here illustrate different ways the fire pit can relate to its surroundings.

ADD SEATING. Permanent stone, wood, or metal bench seats are a practical amenity that turns a fire pit into an inviting destination, even without the attraction of a fire. Seating also acts as a visual clue to identify the spot from a distance.

This contemporary fire pit design is crafted from polished stone blocks.

In addition to reducing the effects of wind on fire, a fire pit has the added benefit of containing the fire glow.

RESOURCE GUIDE

The following list of manufacturers and associations is meant to be a general guide to additional industry and product-related sources. It is not intended as a listing of products and manufacturers represented by the photographs in this book.

AMERICAN NURSERY AND LANDSCAPE ASSOCIATION
(ANLA) offers educational seminars and other services to its members. The Web site offers a way to locate garden centers and landscape designers.
1000 Vermont Ave., NW
Ste. 300
Washington, DC 20015-4914
Phone: 202-789-2900
www.anla.org

ARTISTIC GARDENER offers a number of garden art molds for stepping-stones and benches. Its molds are fully reusable.
421 N.E. Cedar St.
Camas, WA 98607
Phone: 360-834-7021
www.historystones.com

BEUCHEL STONE CORP. provides natural, quarried stone from select cities in the United States. Its product line includes patio stone, accent boulders, and custom-cut stones for steps.
W3639 Hwy. H
Chilton, WI 53014
800-236-4473
www.buechelstone.com

CAST STONE INSTITUTE is a non-profit trade organization that aims to improve the quality of cast stone.
P.O. Box 68
813 Chestnut Street
Lebanon, PA 17042
Phone: 717-272-3744
www.caststone.org

THE COLONIAL STONEYARD specializes in natural stone and stone products for landscaping projects. The company claims that it has the right stone to match anyone's style or budget.
66 North St.
Groton, MA 01450
Phone: 978-448-3329
www.colonialstoneyard.com

CON CRETE FOUNDATIONS ASSOCIATION provides educational materials to contractors in 26 states and Canada.
P.O. Box 204
113 W. First Street
Mt. Vernon, Iowa 52314
Phone: 319-895-6940
www.cfawalls.org

COOLEY STONE offers landscaping options with stone from quarries in northeastern Pennsylvania. The company's Web site offers a complete catalog.
RR 2, Box 154
Kingsley, PA 18826
Phone: 570-278-2355
www.cooleystone.net

THE HEARTH, PATIO, AND BARBECUE ASSOCIATION (HPBA) promotes the hearth products industry.
1901 N. Moore St., Ste. 600
Arlington, Va. 22209
Phone: 703-522-0086
Fax: 703-522-0548
www.hpba.org

HIGH PLAINS STONE provides builders with a selection of building, masonry, and landscape stone from across America. The company's Web site includes a how-to section.
8084 Blakeland Dr.
Littleton, CO 80125
Phone: 303-791-1862
www.highplainsstone.com

HI-TECH ARCHITECTURAL PRODUCTS' Granite Paving division offers a selection of granite and concrete pavers for projects in stone. The company's Web site offers a catalog and free estimates on orders.
www.granitepaving.com

THE INTERNATIONAL MASONRY INSTITUTE provides marketing promotional materials for the masonry industry.
The James Brice House
42 East St.
Annapolis, MD 21401
Phone: 410-280-1305
Fax: 301-261-2855
www.imiweb.org

LANG STONE COMPANY sells home and landscaping stone to professionals and homeowners. The company's Web site features an extensive product gallery.
707 Short St.
Columbus, OH 43215
Phone: 800-589-5264
www.langstone.com

LEARNING STONE offers a number of links to various stone resources. Its Web site also features a stone message board where visitors can read and write posts on the subject of stonework.
www.aboutstone.org

LEMKE STONE, INC., specializes in cobblestone, boulders, Lannon stone, and Bedford stone. The company supplies DIY homeowners as well as professional landscapers, masons, and contractors.
19594 W. Good Hope Rd.
Lannon, WI 53046
Phone: 262-502-1579
www.lemkestone.com

LITTLE MEADOWS STONE COMPANY offers a variety of natural stone for any landscaping project. The company's Web site offers a photo gallery of its product offerings.
RR 1, Box 1324
Friendsville Pa. 18818
Phone: 866-305-3250
www.littlemeadowsstone.com

LOUKONEN BROTHERS STONE produces Colorado red and buff sandstone for builders and landscapers. The Web site features the company's products along with its prices.
12993 N. Foothills Hwy.
Longmont, CO 80503
Phone: 303-823-6268
www.loukonenbros.com

LUCK STONE CORPORATION manufactures a number of construction aggregates and architectural stone. The company's Web site features a product listing and location guide.
P.O. Box 29682
Richmond, VA 23242
Phone: 800-898-5825
www.luckstone.com

MARSHALLTOWN TROWEL COMPANY sells a variety of quality tools to homeowners and masonry professionals.
104 South 8th Ave.
Marshalltown, IA 50158
Phone: 800-888-0127
Fax: 800-477-6341
www.marshalltown.com

THE MASON CONTRACTORS ASSOCIATION OF AMERICA (MCAA) represents mason contractors' needs and promotes the use of masonry through a variety of programs. The organization sells technical manuals dealing with all types of masonry work.
33 S. Roselle Rd.
Schaumberg, IL 60193
Phone: 800-536-2225
www.masoncontractors.org

THE MASONRY ADVISORY COUNCIL provides the public with general and technical information about masonry design and detail. Its Web site contains articles and a guide to brick selection.
1440 Renaissance Dr.
Ste. 302
Park Ridge, IL 60068
Phone: 847-297-6704
www.maconline.org

THE MASONRY SOCIETY is an international group interested in the science, art, and advancement of masonry.
3970 Broadway, Ste. 201-D
Boulder, CO 80304-1135
Phone: 303-939-9700
Fax: 303-541-9215
www.masonrysociety.org

NATIONAL STONE, SAND, AND GRAVEL ASSOCIATION (NSSGA) represents the aggregate industries. Its member companies produce more than 90

percent of the crushed stone used annually in the United States. Visit the association's Web site for workshop and conference information.
1605 King St.
Alexandria, VA 22314
703-525-8788
www.nssga.org

NATURAL-STONE.COM is a Web resource that focuses mostly on the consumer and business-to-business side of the natural stone industry. The Web site has a company locator and a stone search guide.
www.natural-stone.com

NORTHEAST STONE WORKS is the producer of an extensive natural stone line, including boulders, wall stone, and slabs for steps. Visit the company's Web site for more information about its products.
RR 1, Box 1 BB
Springville, PA 18844
Phone: 570-965-2660
www.northeaststone.com

ROLLING ROCK BUILDING STONE, INC., offers its own building products, as well as stone varieties from Asia, Brazil, Canada, and Mexico. Visit the photo gallery at the company's Web site.
40 Rolling Rock Rd.
Boyertown, PA 19512
Phone: 610-987-6226

www.rollrock.com

SELECT STONE, INC., offers natural stone from the United States, as well as Europe and Asia. The company provides stone to residential and commercial construction projects throughout the U.S.
P.O. Box 6403
Bozeman, MT 59771
Phone: 888-237-1000
www.selectstone.com

THE STONE FOUNDATION is a society of stonemasons and others involved with and interested in stone and stonework. Visit its Web site for more information about workshops and symposiums.
116 Lovato Lane
Santa Fe, NM 87505
Phone: 505-989-4644
www.stonefoundation.org

STONE INFO.COM, a division of KD Resources, has a Web site that offers valuable information to construction professionals.
www.stoneinfo.com

STONE WHOLESALE CORPORATION supplies landscape stone, moss rock boulders, and decorative building stone from its own quarry. View the company's Web site for pictures and price lists.
4717 West Lakeview Dr.
Ft. Collins, CO 80526
Phone: 877-221-0057
www.stonewholesalecorp.com

STONE WORLD magazine offers information on stone architecture as well as stone production, distribution, installation, and maintenance. Its Web site offers industry news and a buyer's guide.
BNP Media
210 Route 4 East, Ste. 203
Paramus, NJ 07652
Phone: 201-291-9001
www.stoneworld.com

STONE-X is a directory that promotes the use of natural stone for the construction industry. Stone-X aims at improving business by sharing expertise, knowledge, and experience. Stone-X can be contacted through its Web site.
www.stone-x.com

Metric Equivalents

Length

1 inch	25.4mm
1 foot	0.3048m
1 yard	0.9144m
1 mile	1.61km

Area

1 square inch	645mm^2
1 square foot	0.0929m^2
1 square yard	0.8361m^2
1 acre	4046.86m^2
1 square mile	2.59km^2

Volume

1 cubic inch	16.3870cm^3
1 cubic foot	0.03m^3
1 cubic yard	0.77m^3

Common Lumber Equivalents

Sizes: Metric cross sections are so close to their U.S. sizes, as noted below, that for most purposes they may be considered equivalents.

Dimensional	1 x 2	19 x 38mm
lumber	1 x 4	19 x 89mm
	2 x 2	38 x 38mm
	2 x 4	38 x 89mm
	2 x 6	38 x 140mm
	2 x 8	38 x 184mm
	2 x 10	38 x 235mm
	2 x 12	38 x 286mm
Sheet	4 x 8 ft.	1200 x 2400mm
sizes	4 x 10 ft.	1200 x 3000mm
Sheet	1/4 in.	6mm
thicknesses	3/8 in.	9mm
	1/2 in.	12mm
	3/4 in.	19mm
Stud/joist	16 in. o.c.	400mm o.c.
spacing	24 in. o.c.	600mm o.c.

Capacity

1 fluid ounce	29.57mL
1 pint	473.18mL
1 quart	0.95L
1 gallon	3.79L

Weight

1 ounce	28.35g
1 pound	0.45kg

Temperature

Fahrenheit = Celsius x 1.8 + 32
Celsius = Fahrenheit - 32 x $\frac{5}{9}$

Nail Size and Length

Penny Size	Nail Length
2d	1"
3d	1¼"
4d	1½"
5d	1¾"
6d	2"
7d	2¼"
8d	2½"
9d	2¾"
10d	3"
12d	3¼"
16d	3½"

GLOSSARY

AGGREGATE Crushed stone, gravel, or other material added to cement to make concrete or mortar. Gravel and crushed stone are considered coarse aggregate; sand is considered fine aggregate.

ASHLAR Any stone cut to a square or rectangular shape in either random or uniform sizes. Also, a pattern for laying courses of rectangular blocks of stone.

BACKFILL Sand, gravel, pea stone, or crushed stone used to refill excavated areas with a stable, porous material.

BATTER The angle or slope of a stone wall from base to top that is necessary for stability.

BED Horizontal masonry joint, sometimes called bed joint. Also, any prepared surface (stone, gravel, sand, or mortar) for placing stone.

BELGIAN BLOCKS Stone cut in square or rectangular shapes, usually about the size of a large brick, and used for paving.

BONDSTONE A long stone used to tie the wythes together in a freestanding wall. Sometimes called a through stone.

BUILDING SURFACE The faces or surfaces of a stone that carry and distribute the load in a wall, typically the surfaces that are the top and bottom of a wall stone.

CAPSTONES Stone used to form the top course of a wall.

CHINKERS Small, irregularly shaped stones used to fill gaps in a wall.

COBBLESTONE Any small-dimension milled stone that is used for paving.

CONCRETE A mixture of portland cement, sand, gravel or crushed rock, and water that forms a solid material when cured.

COPING The top layer of stones on a wall, usually slightly wider than the wall, sometimes called capstones. Also, the individual stones that make up the finished edge around a pond or pool.

COURSES The horizontal layers of stones in a wall. Also, the rows of uniform-sized stone or pavers used to make a walk or patio.

CRAZY PAVING Irregularly shaped pieces of stone used to make a walk or patio.

CRUSHED ROCK Small-dimension material available in a range of colors and sizes with rough, angular surfaces.

CURING The process by which concrete becomes solid and develops strength.

CUT STONE Any stone that has been milled or worked by hand to a specific shape or dimensions.

DRESSED STONE Usually quarried stone that has been squared-off on all sides and has a smooth face.

DRY WALL A stone wall constructed without mortar.

EXCAVATION To remove earth or soil so that the construction will be supported by a subgrade that is hard, uniformly graded, and well drained.

FACE The exposed side of a stone.

FIELDSTONE Stone as it is found in the natural environment.

FLAGGING Paving for walks or patios made from flagstone.

FLAGSTONE Any stone milled to a uniform thickness of 1 to 2 inches to use for walk and patio surfaces. Flagstone is available in uniform rectangular shapes or in random-shaped pieces sometimes called crazy paving.

FOOTING Support for mortared stonework generally made of concrete and extending below the frost line to avoid problems from frost heaves.

FROST HEAVE Shifting or upheaval of the ground resulting from alternate freezing and thawing of water in the soil.

FROST LINE The maximum depth to which soil freezes in the winter. Frost line depth varies from region to region and is deeper under areas that are cleared of snow in winter, such as walkways, steps, and driveways.

GROUND-FAULT CIRCUIT INTERRUPTER (GFCI) A safety circuit breaker that compares the amount of current entering a receptacle with the amount leaving it. If there is a discrepancy, the GFCI breaks the circuit and stops the current. The device is required by electrical code in areas that are subject to dampness.

HARDSCAPE That portion of a landscape that is made of nonliving material, such as concrete, stone, or lumber.

MASON'S LINE A type of twine used by masons that can be stretched taut. It is used to lay out projects, check for level, and as a straightedge guide to check the evenness of a course as it is being laid.

MICROCLIMATE An area in a landscape with growing conditions that differ from the rest of the landscape. The differences can be caused by variances in the amount of sunlight received, wind currents, topography, and other factors.

MORTAR A mixture of cementitious materials, fine aggregate, and water. Mortar is used to bond bricks or blocks.

NOMINAL DIMENSIONS The dimensions of a masonry unit plus one mortar joint.

PEA GRAVEL Small rounded stone most often used in gravel gardens or for walkways.

PORTLAND CEMENT A mixture of burned lime, iron, silica, and alumina. This mixture is put through a kiln, ground into a fine powder, and packaged for sale.

PREPACKAGED CONCRETE MIX A mix that combines cement, sand, and gravel in the correct proportions and requires only the addition of water to create fresh concrete.

READY-MIX CONCRETE Wet concrete that is transported from a concrete supplier. The concrete is ready to pour.

REBAR Reinforcing bar that is used for concrete that will carry a heavy load, such as footings, foundation walls, columns, and pilasters.

RETAINING WALLS A wall built to hold back sloping ground or make a grade change. Retaining walls can be dry-laid or mortared.

PAVERS Any stone milled to a uniform size and shape, typically about the size of a brick, and used to surface walkways and patios.

QUARRY DRESSED Stone that is squared-off on all sides but has a rough face. Sometimes called semidressed stone.

RIVERSTONES Small- to medium-size stones that are worn or rounded from water.

ROUGH STONE Stone as it comes from the quarry.

SCREEDING Moving a straight board, such as a 2x4, back and forth across the tops of forms to smooth and level sand or concrete.

STAND-ALONE FOUNTAIN A fountain that has its own reservoir and does not require a pond. (Also called a self-contained fountain.)

STEEL REINFORCEMENT Reinforcing mesh or rebar that is used to strengthen concrete.

TAMP Compacting gravel or sand in 2- to 4-inch layers to form a solid base for flat stonework, such as a patio.

TAMPER A hand tool or power device used to compact soil or gravel so that it is less likely to shift or crumble.

THROUGH STONE A long stone used to tie the wythes together in a freestanding wall. Sometimes called a bondstone.

TOPSOIL The uppermost layer of soil; it is the most fertile and workable for gardeners.

WEEP HOLE A hole in a mortared retaining wall that allows water to seep through to relieve pressure against the wall. Typically formed by embedding a length of plastic or metal pipe in a mortar joint.

WYTHE The vertical section of a wall that is one stone or one masonry unit wide.

INDEX

TECHNICAL EDITOR

Mark Wolfe is a garden and landscape content specialist based in Georgia, with an extensive background in the green industry. He works as an industry expert and commerce writer at BobVila.com, while contributing content and editing services for many other outlets. Mark graduated from Northland College in Ashland, Wisconsin with a degree in outdoor education. Early in his career, Mark fell in love with plants. Working on stream restoration and wetlands construction projects, he marveled at the willow's ability to quickly grow from a stem fragment and heal a sorely eroded streambank, and the ways that aquatic plants transform a suburban retention pond into a wildlife oasis. Over the next two decades, trees, shrubs, annuals, and perennials would dominate his working life as a landscaper and nursery manager. In the mid-twenty-teens, Mark co-founded a garden blog, ThePrudentGarden.com, and soon began contributing freelance work for dozens of lawn and garden websites and consumer brands. As a writer, his favorite topics are those that help those who are new to plants and gardening find success and helping seasoned plant people find new inspiration. As a gardener, he is passionate about establishing backyard habitats for wild birds and pollinators and growing his collection of native azaleas.

CREDITS

CH = Creative Homeowner; SS = Shutterstock.com

pages 4–5: *all* Harpur Garden Images **page 6:** Mark Lohman, design: Design Line Interiors, Inc. **pages 7–9:** *all* Mark Lohman pages 10–11: *all* Harpur Garden Images **page 12:** *top* Harpur Garden Images; *bottom* Jessie Walker **page 13:** Anne Gummerson **page 14:** Jessie Walker **page 15:** John Glover **pages 16–17:** *all* Harpur Garden Images **page 18:** *top* Ken Druse; *bottom* Mark Lohman **page 19:** Mark Lohman **page 20:** *all* Alan & Linda Detrick; **page 21:** *top* Alan & Linda Detrick; *bottom* Michael S. Thompson **pages 22–26:** *all* Harpur Garden Images **page 27:** *all* Anne Gummerson **page 28:** *top left* Mark Lohman, architect: Burdge & Associates Architects, Inc.; *top right and bottom* Anne Gummerson **page 29:** Harpur Garden Images **page 30:** Brian Vanden Brink, architect: John Morris **page 31:** *top* Brian Vanden Brink Photos/Todd Caverly; *bottom* Brian Vanden Brink, design: Horiuchi & Solien Landscape **page 32:** *right* Harpur Garden Images; *bottom left* Walter Chandoha **page 33:** *top* Mark Lohman; *bottom right* Jerry Pavia; *bottom left* Mark Lohman **page 34:** Harpur Garden Images **page 35:** *top left and bottom right* Jerry Pavia; *top right* Tony Giammarino/Giammarino Dworkin, design: Maymont Gardens; *bottom left* Brian Vanden Brink **page 36:** *top* Mark Lohman; *bottom* Harpur Garden Images **page 37:** *all* Mark Lohman **page 38:** *all* Harpur Garden Images **page 39:** *top* Harpur Garden Images; *bottom right* Mark Lohman; *bottom left* Jessie Walker **pages 40–41:** *all* Mark Lohman **page 42:** Michael S. Thompson **page 43:** Mark Lohman **pages 44:** Mark Lohman **pages 45–46:** *all* Anne Gummerson **page 47:** Mark Lohman **pages 48-49:** *all* Mark Lohman **pages 50–51:** *all* Mark Lohman **page 52:** Harpur Garden Images **page 53:** John Parsekian/CH **page 54:** Mark Lohman **page 55:** *top left and top right* Mark Lohman, design: Roxanne Packham Design; *bottom* Anne Gummerson **page 56:** Mark Lohman, architect: Burdge & Associates Architects, Inc **page 57:** Mark Lohman page 58: *top, middle, and bottom* Debbie Wolf; *bottom inset* Irina Barilo/SS **page 59:** *top, middle, and bottom* Debbie Wolf; *top inset* Keithster22/SS; *bottom inset* charles taylor/SS **page 60:** *top, middle, and bottom* Debbie Wolf; *middle inset* TAMER YILMAZ/SS **page 61:** *top, middle, and bottom* Debbie Wolf; *top inset* Oleg 08/SS **pages 62–63:** *all* Debbie Wolf **pages 64:** *bottom left* Charles Mann; *middle right* Mark Lohman **page 65:** Mark Lohman **page 66:** Harpur Garden Image **page 67:** diagram udaya fire/SS; photo

Ivonne Wierink/SS **page 68:** Harpur Garden Images **page 69:** Mark Lohman **page 70:** *all* John Parsekian/CH; **page 71:** *top* John Parsekian/CH; *bottom* Brian C. Nieves/CH **page 72:** Mark Lohman **page 73:** Mark Lohman **pages 74–75:** Harpur Garden Images **page 77:** *top* Anne Gummerson; *bottom all* John Parsekian/CH **page 78:** Mark Lohman **page 79:** *top* Mark Lohman; *bottom* Anne Gummerson **page 80:** Mark Lohman **page 81:** Mark Lohman **page 82:** Harpur Garden Images **page 83:** Anne Gummerson **page 84:** Mark Lohman **page 85:** Harpur Garden Images **page 86:** Red Cover **page 87:** Anne Gummerson **page 88:** *top* Anne Gummerson; *bottom* Harpur Garden Images **pages 89–90:** Jessie Walker **page 92:** Anne Gummerson **page 93:** Harpur Garden Images **page 94:** *bottom left* Jerry Pavia; *middle right* Ingrid Balabanova/SS **page 95:** Harpur Garden Images **page 97:** Jerry Pavia **page 98:** Harpur Garden Images **page 99:** *top* Ken Druse; *bottom* Merle Henkenius **pages 100–101:** *all* Mark Lohman **page 102:** *top and bottom left* John Parsekian/CH; *bottom right* Jessie Walker **page 103:** Jessie Walker **pages 105–107:** *all* Harpur Garden Images **page 108:** Jessie Walker pages **110–111:** *top left* Mark Lohman; *bottom left* Jessie Walker; *center* Anne Gummerson; *right* John Parsekian/CH **page 112:** *top* John Parsekian/CH; *bottom* Mark Samu **page 113:** *top* Anne Gummerson; *bottom* Harpur Garden Images **page 115:** Mark Lohman, design: Design Line Interiors, Inc. **page 116:** *top* John Parsekian/CH; *bottom* Red Cover **page 117:** Harpur Garden Images **pages 118–119:** *top* Jessie Walker; *bottom* Harpur Garden Images **page 120:** Mark Lohman **page 121:** *all* Red Cover **pages 123–125:** *all* Harpur Garden Images **pages 126–127:** *left* Harpur Garden Images; *right* Red Cover **page 128:** Jessie Walker **page 129:** Red Cover **pages 130–131:** *all* Jessie Walker **page 132:** Mark Lohman **page 133:** *top* Harpur Garden Images; *bottom* Carolyn L. Bates, design & installation: Paul Wieczoreck, Champlain Valley Landscaping **page 134:** *all* Anne Gummerson **page 135:** Harpur Garden Images **pages 136–137:** *all* Red Cover **pages 138–139:** *left* Harpur Garden Images; *right* David Cavagnaro **page 140:** *top* David Cavagnaro; *bottom* John Glover **pages 141–143:** *all* Debbie Wolfe **pages 144–146:** *all* Red Cover **pages 147–148:** *all* David Cavagnaro **page 149:** *left* Red Cover; *right* David Cavagnaro **pages 150–151:** *left* Red Cover; *right* Harpur Garden Images **page 152:** Harpur Garden

Images **page 153:** Carolyn L. Bates, design & installation: Andrea Morgante Landscaping **page 154:** Carolyn L. Bates, design & installation: Thomas Vanacore **page 155:** Harpur Garden Images **page 156:** Charles Mann **page 157:** *top* Harpur Garden Images; *bottom* Charles Mann **pages 158–160:** Harpur Garden Images **page 161:** Charles Mann **page 162:** *top* Charles Mann; *bottom* Jessie Walker **page 166:** Red Cover **page 167:** Brian Vanden Brink **page 168:** *top* David Cavagnaro; *bottom* Carolyn L. Bates **page 169:** Mark Lohman **pages 170–172:** *all* Red Cover **page 173:** Werner Spremberg/SS **page 174:** Harpur Garden Images **page 175:** Ken Druse **page 176:** Red Cover **page 177:** David Cavagnaro **page 178:** Red Cover **page 179:** *all* David Cavagnaro **page 180:** *(top row, all)* Galen Gates; *(bottom row, left to right)* Dembinsky Photo Associates/Richard Shiell; Susan A. Roth; David Cavagnaro; John Glover; John Glover **page 181:** *(top row, left to right)* John Glover; Photo Researchers/Norm Thomas; Photo Researchers/E.R. Degginger; *bottom row* John Glover; Positive Images/Margaret Hensel; John Glover; *right* Rob Cardillo **pages 182–183:** *left* Mark Lohman, design: Stout Landscaping; *right* Jessie Walker **page 184:** Jessie Walker **page 185:** Todd Caverly **page 186:** Harpur Garden Images **page 187:** Todd Caverly **page 189:** Jessie Walker **page 190:** *top* John Parsekian/CH; *bottom* Jessie Walker **page 191:** Mark Lohman **page 192:** Tony Giammarino/Giammarino Dworkin **page 193:** *top* Jessie *Walker;* *bottom right* Tony Giammarino/Giammarino Dworkin; *bottom left* Alan & Linda *Detrick* **page 195:** Red Cover **page 196:** *top* John Parsekian/CH; *bottom right* Red Cover; *bottom left* John Parsekian/CH **page 197:** Mark Lohman **pages 198–199:** *all* Charles Mann **page 200:** *top* Charles Mann; *bottom* Carolyn L. Bates, *design & installation:* Paul Wieczoreck, Champlain Valley Landscaping **page 201:** Mark Samu **page 202:** Mark Lohman, design: Stout Landscaping **pages 203–204:** *all* Charles Mann **page 205:** *top and center* John Parsekian/CH; *bottom* Mark Lohman, design: Maraya Droney Design **page 206:** Mark Samu **page 207:** *top* Mark Lohman, design: Maraya Droney Design; *bottom* Charles Mann **page 208:** Harpur Garden Images **page 209:** Mark Lohman **page 210:** Harpur Garden Images **pages 211–212:** Mark Lohman **page 213:** Anne Gummerson **page 214:** Harpur Garden Images **page 221:** Mark Lohman

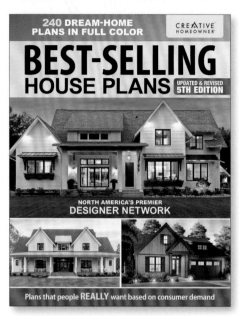
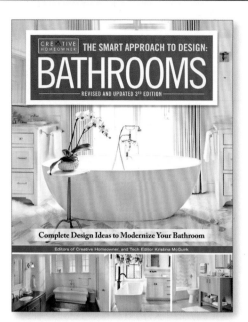
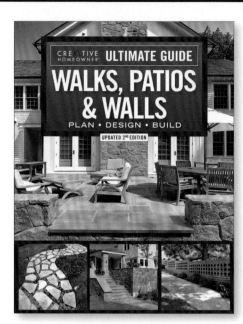
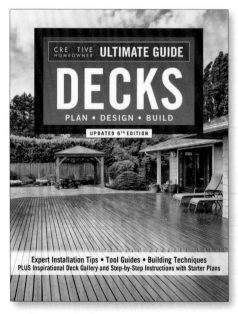

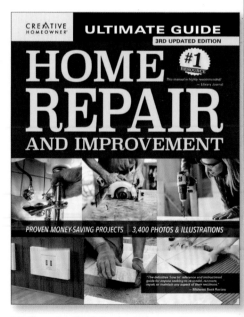